SUPPER WITH THE PRE

Ian Mathie spent his childhood and early school years in Africa. After a short service commission in the RAF, he returned to the continent as a rural development officer working for the British government and a number of other agencies. His work in water resources and related projects during the 1970s brought him into close contact with the African people, their cultures and varied tribal customs, many of which are now all but lost. These experiences, recorded in his notebooks, were the inspiration for a series of African memoirs, of which *Supper with the President* is the third volume. Ian continued to visit Africa until health considerations curtailed his travelling. He now lives in south Warwickshire with his wife and dog.

By the same author

SUPPER WITH THE PRESIDENT

*For Peggy,
with Best Wishes*

Ian Mathie

Ian Mathie

MOSAÏQUEPRESS

First published in the UK in 2011 by
MOSAÏQUE PRESS
Registered office:
70 Priory Road
Kenilworth, Warwickshire CV8 1LQ
www.mosaïquepress.co.uk

Cover design by Gary Henderson
GH Graphic Design Ltd

Printed in the UK.

ISBN 978-1-906852-10-8

For Gay

Maps

Contents

The line of duty: From the right, the Russian, French and East German diplomats attending the inauguration, alongside representatives of other foreign governments. The President is seated just beyond the empty chair, which was re-occupied by the author after he took this photo.

1 ~ Moussa's mud pile

THE RUSSIAN AMBASSADOR was seething, his French counterpart stared rigorously into space while the East German *chef de mission* was simply baffled. The day was hot, the air grey with dust. Their collars were biting and, what was worse, they had been seated at the edge of the dais. How, when each made it his business to know in detail what the others were up to, were they going to explain to their governments back home that a major development project had reached fruition in front of their noses and none of them had played any part in it?

Diplomacy at the best of times is a game of endless intrigues. In newly evolving 1970s Africa, spies followed spies in a clandestine conga. Seeking influence and patronage, the world's diplomatic corps, or at least that part of it that was represented in Bamako at the time, were so wrapped up in their great game that they missed quite obvious opportunities to do something worthwhile that might have helped them achieve their aims.

But there we were, assembled at a location halfway to nowhere to celebrate a major success of the regime. It would not have entered the consciousness of these constantly scheming diplomats

Republic of Mali showing the site of the mud dam.

that pure chance might have had anything to do with it, but chance coupled with the observations of a fresh eye and a word in the right ear was the delicious truth of the matter. And where was HMG's representative? Not there...

COMING FROM THE SOUTH towards Bamako, I had been unlucky enough to get three punctures within a couple of hours. Although I always carried two spare wheels in my Land Rover, falling victim to a sharp-edged pot-hole a third time effectively brought my trip to a complete halt until I carried out repairs. Luck, however, was not all against me, for when that third tyre popped on the Sinkisso road, I was only half a kilometre from a good sized village. I could see several trucks stopped by the roadside and plenty of people milling around them, so there was a good chance that I could find a mechanic in the village who would help me mend at least one of the flat tyres.

I lifted one of the damaged wheels from the back and set off towards the village, rolling the wheel along like a small boy. It didn't take long to find someone able and willing to fix it and when he heard that I had two other punctures, he offered to mend those as well if I brought the wheels to him. I returned to the Land Rover, jacked it up and removed the wheel with the puncture, then lowered the jack to let the vehicle's back axle sit on a large stone that I collected from the roadside.

When I returned with the other two wheels, the mechanic told me it would take at least an hour to mend them all, so I set off to explore the village. Unlike most roadside villages, which sprawled along on both sides of the highway, most of this village was set off to one side and only a few huts and shops were clustered along the road front. The rest of the village was on ground that sloped down, away from the road, overlooking a narrow valley that opened into a wide flat pan where a few fields of maize and millet were planted. The land in the valley was scattered with numerous termite castles, standing like steep red spires, five or six feet tall. It was curious that there were none in the pan and, having time to waste, I wandered down there to have a look.

No obvious explanation for this phenomenon presented itself, but looking up towards the valley gave me an idea. The valley neck offered the ideal site to place a small earth dam that could catch the runoff from the slopes in the wet season and hold it back for use to irrigate the whole of this pan. Presently less than a quarter of the pan was cultivated. The ground looked ideal for growing vegetables and I could easily imagine a huge market garden laid out here. I went back to my vehicle for a soil testing kit and spent half an hour taking soil samples and playing with chemicals. This, of course, attracted a small crowd of curious children, who accompanied me wherever I went, chattering brightly amongst themselves and occasionally to me.

I wandered up into the valley to look at the ground there and found that just above the village there was indeed an ideal site for a dam. I had no means of digging to investigate what was below the surface, but there were a number of large rocks protruding that had all the characteristics of being outcrops of an underground stratum and not just loose boulders. It seemed likely, therefore, that there would be a firm base to which an earth dam could be anchored. The concept continued to grow in my mind and I was soon aware of that excitement that comes when you find the potential for a really worthwhile development project.

Most of the trucks had moved on by the time I returned to the village. The mechanic was working on my third tyre. I took one that he had already fixed, returned to the Land Rover and fitted it, then drove back to the village and parked next to his *atelier*. I sat and chatted with the mechanic while he worked and asked him about the village and the valley. Other people, curious to see a stranger in their village, came along to look and to listen and soon joined it the conversation.

"Do you ever grow any other crops on the flat pan below the valley?" I asked in the course of the discussion. A general shaking of heads was my answer. Someone offered that there was not enough water to support anything more than a small amount of millet or maize, even in the wet season. The water rushed down from the slopes so fast that it was gone before it had time to soak into the fields.

"Why haven't you built a dam to hold the water back?" I asked.

"If anyone tried that the government would only come and interfere," someone remarked.

I said, rather jokingly, that when I got to Bamako I would go to the President's office and ask for permission, and maybe even some help, to build a dam. Everyone laughed; nobody ever got to see the President, they said, and he would not be interested in their little village.

My final wheel was mended, so I paid my bill, said goodbye to these friendly people and, promising to stop there again next time I came along this road, I headed for the capital. As I was leaving one of the men who had joined our discussion called out, "Have a nice visit to the President!"

"I will," I called back, "In fact I will invite him to come down here and give you the permission himself!" They laughed and waved me goodbye.

When I got to Bamako, I had meetings with a number of people including the local representatives of several UN agencies. One was a Cypriot called Andras Patsakis. I hadn't met him before but we got along famously from the first moment. He was also an irrigation engineer by training, so when I mentioned my idea about a dam and a market garden, he was immediately interested. He invited me to dine with him that evening, saying he had at least one Malian guest coming who would be very interested in my idea.

At dinner that evening I was seated next to a charming fellow whom Andras introduced as Ousmane Baba, adding that he was someone with 'influence' who would be keen to hear about my idea. He was indeed interested, and asked all sorts of searching questions. I found myself pulling out a pen and drawing diagrams of the valley and the pan on my double damask dinner napkin. On the other side I drew sketches of how the dam might be built and scribbled notes about irrigation channels and sluice gates. I had drawn a few similar notes on paper earlier in Andras's office, but now I got slightly carried away with the idea and developed it in more detail.

Ousmane Baba was particularly interested in my idea about how this scheme, and other similar projects, could be realised at minimal cost and to the general benefit of the country. Again he asked many searching questions and before the evening was over, he had invited me to dine at his own house the following evening, saying that he would invite his cousin to come as well. He was sure that his cousin would not only be very interested in my ideas but, Ousmane assured me, he had the influence necessary to make sure it got a hearing in the right government circles. He was a man who could make things happen. I'd heard that one before, but there was no harm in trying, so I accepted the invitation.

As we rose from the dinner table, I failed to notice that my dinner companion had sequestered the napkin and folded it into the pocket of his robe. I was therefore a little taken aback the following evening when he introduced me to his cousin, Moussa, and handed him the napkin. "You should get Ian to tell you about this idea of his," said Ousmane, "particularly about how he thinks it should be built."

Moussa was a charming man, a few years older than his cousin, who had obviously already told him the essence of my crazy plan. He proceeded to quiz me in detail about the whole idea and what had prompted it. He also wanted me to explain precisely what I proposed as a means of executing the plan, which was a little unconventional and would involve the army.

I have always kept my nose well out of politics in Africa. This has generally meant that even in countries which have had coups and revolutions, I have been able to continue my work unimpeded. Rural development should, after all, be a non-political business. This non-involvement, however, does not imply that I remained unaware of what was going on; of the political pressures, trends and influential parties, or of the influence that the army so often exerted. Since many of the region's countries were run by military regimes, some understanding of this aspect was essential. Mali was no exception to this, the current President having snatched control by a military coup in November 1968. He was reputed to have disposed of a number of political opponents, either by shooting them or by exiling them as slave labour to the salt mines at Taoudéni in the far north. He still held the country in an iron grip.

I was also well aware of the fragility of some governmental institutions in many African states. Stability was necessary for development. It was this understanding that had prompted my ideas about getting this project achieved by using the army to do the construction work. Some of the rumble of low level political unrest in Mali emanated from military officers with too much time on their hands and not enough to occupy them. There had been a number of purges to counter this in recent years, but the unrest was still there, simmering away below the surface; a pot near the boil with the lid jammed on tight.

It occurred to me that the army's engineers, who had earth moving equipment, could be usefully deployed to move a bit of earth and create the dam. Other soldiers could be used for other tasks, like digging irrigation ditches and removing termite colonies to improve the land, and in a very short time the job could be done, well before the next rainy season.

The military personnel were already employed and being paid, but they spent most of their time lounging around in barracks with nothing to do. Potentially they were a fertile field in which to plant the seeds of revolution but, if occupied with a civil engineering project and able to see the results of their labours, this risk could be reduced. "If the pan below the dam could be developed for market gardening, it should be able to produce enough vegetables not only for the villagers' needs, but to supply a lot to the army barracks as well," I reasoned. "This could improve the soldiers' diet and help morale."

The whole idea, and particularly the bit about getting the army engineers to do the work, appealed to Moussa and he said that he would propose it to friends in the government who, he felt sure, could make it possible. I told him that if the Malian army could help with this project I would make sure that funds were provided by my employer, the British government, to pay for the diesel their bulldozers would consume. With a beaming smile he said he would tell the Commander in Chief to send me the fuel bill.

Before Ousmane's car took me back to my hotel, Moussa asked about my programme for the next few weeks. I told him that I was due to leave for Senegal the next day by train and expected to fly back to Mali in about six weeks time. He gave me a small pasteboard card bearing nothing but his name, Moussa, and a telephone number, and asked me to call him from the airport the minute I arrived back in Bamako. He would have me picked up and we could discuss this idea further. When I returned to my hotel, the concierge told me that someone called Moussa had telephoned, asking for the number of my return flight. If I would care to leave it at the desk, he would pass it on when the caller rang back next day.

I gave him the details, went to bed, slept soundly and next morning caught the early train to Dakar, reflecting that it had been an enjoyable evening, it would be nice to think something might come of my scheme, but this was Africa. I had learned long ago not to have expectations that were too grand. The idea of building a dam might get discussed with a few government officials, but it was unlikely that the army would even give it a hearing. Never mind, I would stop at the village after I came back, on my way down to Sinkisso, and talk to the villagers to see if there might be another way of doing the job, as I really did think it would be worthwhile. Meanwhile, Senegal called.

THERE WERE FIVE PROJECTS running in Senegal that demanded my attention and a number of new ideas to be explored. The six weeks soon passed and I gave almost no thought to the idea about a dam in Mali until my flight was descending towards Bamako airport. Then I remembered Moussa's insistence that I should call him from the terminal and he would get me picked up. It took a moment to locate his card in my notebook and, as soon as I had cleared immigration and customs, I went looking for a telephone.

There were no public phones anywhere, but I managed to persuade a chap in one of the airline offices to let me make the call from his office on the promise that I would book my flight through him next time I needed to fly to Senegal. I didn't tell him that I normally used my own aeroplane and had only used the airline this time because it was being overhauled.

Moussa's phone was answered by a woman who told me to wait where I was, that she would pass on the message and someone would collect me within about twenty minutes. She sounded efficient and friendly and I felt relaxed about waiting. I looked at my wristwatch as I went outside and sat on my case, watching the other passengers and all the people who had come to assist their comings and goings.

Twenty minutes later, a shiny Mercedes drew up and a driver in smart green trousers with matching shirt emerged from the driving seat. It was almost like a military uniform, but carried no insignia or badges. Whoever Moussa was, it was plain that he could afford a smart car and driver to match. The driver asked me to climb in, put my suitcase in the boot, and drove off. Almost immediately we turned off the normal route and took a small side road that led around the back of the terminal building. It took us to the military side of the airport. The driver pulled up by an old Russian Mi-4 helicopter in Malian military markings. He climbed out, opened the door for me, told me to leave my luggage in the car and climb aboard the helicopter through the open rear hatch.

To my surprise, Moussa was already seated in the helicopter, chatting to a man wearing a colonel's insignia. He greeted me and motioned me to take a seat by the window. The pilot started the engines immediately and any attempt to ask Moussa what was going on was drowned by the noise. When the helicopter was airborne, a crewman handed an intercom headset to each of us. It was a relief to put it on and have the racket deadened slightly, and it made communication possible.

Before I could ask what this was all about, Moussa told me that it had been arranged for him to take me on a visit to the proposed site of the dam that I had talked about, so that he could get a clearer idea of the extent of the project. I realised that a hasty rethink of my previous scepticism about this man was called for. Quite clearly Moussa did have influence and maybe he really could make things happen.

After only fifteen minutes flying, the helicopter started to circle and Moussa pointed out of the window, asking me if we had come to the correct place. Being a military helicopter, the Mi-4's windows were small and round, not made for sightseeing, and I had to crane my head to see anything. Below I could make out the road and the village, but something was very different from what I remembered seeing on the ground.

As we continued round, I saw raw earth, then a dam across the valley. Water was already beginning to collect behind the dam and, as far as I could see through the small porthole, it would eventually make a lake about two kilometres long in the narrow valley. Below the dam there was a series of channels and a number of tractors and other machines shaping and ploughing the land. I thought we must have come to another project for comparison.

The helicopter did two circuits and then landed on the outskirts of the village. As the door opened and we climbed out, I recognised the village. It was the one I had stopped at, but where had that dam come from? I was sure it hadn't been there before and they could hardly have built it in the short time I had been away in Senegal. My amazement must have shown on my face.

"Have we done what you intended?" Moussa asked me.

"Yes, but how did this happen? It is absolutely amazing," I said, still finding it difficult to believe.

"Many things are possible if you have the right influence," Moussa replied. "By the way, you promised to pay for the fuel for the machinery; you had better have this." He handed me a bill for 8,760,000 Malian francs – about £7,300.

"What do you mean by the right influence?" I asked.

Before he could answer, my mechanic friend from the village forced his way though the crowd. He came over and shook my hand.

"I thought you were joking when you told me you would ask the President to help us build a dam," he said.

"I was," I told him.

"So who is this?" he asked, indicating Moussa.

I looked at my companion and raised an eyebrow.

"Yes," he said, almost sheepishly "I am Moussa Traoré, Président de la République."

The fuel bill was well within the limit of my discretionary account so I went to the bank the next morning, arranged a bank draft for the full amount and took it round to the President's office. That evening I was invited to supper with the President again, but this time, at least, I knew who he was.

WHEN I SUBMITTED the receipt to London, my boss – a self-important and naturally suspicious man named Gerald – had apoplexy. I had until then not spent any of the discretionary funds to which I had access and London wanted to know why I had done so this time and on the basis of very little information passed back to them. After a brief and terse exchange of telexes, Gerald decided to come to Mali to see for himself what sort of a mud pile 'Mad Mathie' had spent the taxpayers' money on.

When he arrived in Bamako, Gerald just wanted to see the dam and go back to London but the Malians were determined to get the most out of his presence and laid on visits and inspections of

An impressive structure: Gerald (left) takes in the view below the dam with the author.

everything but the dam. He had been in the country four days before he finally got to see it, and that was only after Colonel Ouada, the man in charge of the engineers regiment that had built it, had made his own staff car available to take us there with a full military escort.

The construction work had been completed months earlier and the main rains had filled the lake behind the dam. The open surface of the huge earth dyke was scarred by numerous small channels where heavy rain had started to carve its face, but these were only minor erosion gullies which would be repaired and planted with grass and stabilising shrubs before the next rains.

It was an impressive structure; even Gerald was awed by its size. The field network below the dam was lush and green with crops ripening. Baskets of tomatoes, okra, beans and other vegetables were being brought up to the village for onward carriage by road to the military barracks at Bamako.

We stood on the face of the dam, looking out over the fields below and admired the scale of work that had been done for so little cost. "So what's the catch?" Gerald demanded. In his mind, everything had a catch.

"Catch? What do you mean?"

"It's not possible to build a dam this size for £7,400. Where's the rest of the cost coming from?"

"There is no rest of the cost," I told him. "You've read my report. Someone passed my idea on to a man who could make things happen and because I said we would pay the fuel bill if the Malian army did the work, the army did it and used that amount of fuel. That's it. No other costs, no wages to pay, no bribes, no kick-backs. The man with influence made it happen."

Gerald was still finding it difficult to get his head around this. "Okay, so who is this mysterious mate of yours who can make things happen?"

"Moussa? Oh, he's the President."

That was the only time I ever saw Gerald speechless. His mouth opened and closed but no words came out. I left him to play carp and went to talk to the tyre mender who had inspired the original idea.

I put Gerald on the plane to Paris the following morning. Driving him to the airport, I could almost hear the cogwheels grinding in his head. He was working out how to explain this unconventional project to the finance committee and needed an extra something to justify his approval of what he had previously described as a madcap scheme.

"Just one last question," he began. "How many people live in that village beside the dam?"

"Roughly a thousand," I said. "That makes it under eight quid a head to feed them all for the next ten years or more. I hope you find that good value for money."

He thought about this for a moment and then I saw him smile. "And an idle army is a liability in a country like this," he added, "but give them something to do and the prospect of a gain from that activity and they're less likely to make trouble. I take it they'll get most of the food grown on that farm?"

I nodded.

"You devious, cunning sod."

I took this as a compliment.

A couple of months later when I picked up my mail from the post office in Ouahigouya, I found a letter from Peter Akende, a Ghanaian friend who worked in our accounts department in London. "I thought you might be interested to know," he wrote, "that Gerald's recent trip to visit you cost the taxpayers £7,718."

REGIMES COME AND GO in Africa and eventually, in March 1991, Moussa Traoré was replaced as President by General Ahmadu Touré, who mounted a military coup on the tail of violently suppressed student demonstrations. The dam was not quite as durable as Moussa Traoré's regime because, unfortunately, the military engineers had been a little lax about following the 'plans', such as they were. They didn't key the footing into the bed of the valley effectively and eventually it failed. Long before that happened, the structure had been weakened by erosion from the annual rains which ate into the surface of the dam. The roots of bushes and grass that had been planted under a different project held it at bay for a few years while also providing forage for the village goats.

Even so the dam managed to irrigate nearly eight hundred hectares of vegetable gardens for nine consecutive years until, through lack of maintenance and heavy rain, seepage into the foundations caused the dam to collapse and covered most of the cultivated area with thick red mud. Fortunately the collapse happened at night and nobody was hurt in the flood. The army had completely lost interest by this time and, although the villagers tried to rebuild a small dam, it never amounted to much and they returned to tilling patches of millet and maize, harvesting mangoes and oranges from trees planted long ago by their former colonial masters, and selling fruit to passing traffic.

2 ~ Mint tea and
a one-eyed goat

I HAD BEEN IN BAMAKO for nearly a week and was due to travel west into Senegal when my vehicle was involved in a spectacular smash. Fortunately I wasn't in it at the time and nobody was hurt, but it did mean that the old crate had to go to a workshop for some major repairs and would be off the road for at least four weeks. Quite aside from parts being less than easy to get in Mali, the mechanics were not the fastest operators in the world. There was no point in harassing them in the hope of getting the job done any sooner and no other vehicle suitable for the rugged trip I needed to make was available. The only alternative was to take the twice-weekly train to Dakar and source another vehicle when I arrived. I went down to the railway station to buy a ticket.

The booking clerk was adamant that I could only travel first class and that I should be accommodated in a sleeper carriage. The first of that week's trains had departed about half an hour earlier and it would still be possible to catch up and board as it would not yet have done more than ten kilometres. Sadly, however, it had been fully booked, so I would have to wait for the next one, which was not due to depart for three days. There was nothing for it but to book now and find something else to do in Bamako for a couple of days.

My ticket cost 12,955 Malian francs and the sleeper car, together with all meals served during the journey, cost a further 3,675 francs. This grand total of 16,630 francs translated to £13.85. This was for more than a thousand miles of 'luxury' travel. Train number two was due to leave at 0810 on 28 May, with me in berth number two of First Class Carriage B. As there were two berths per compartment, I would be sharing with somebody whose identity I would not discover until we boarded – normal for West African public transport.

Back in the city, I spent a couple of days exploring parts of it I had not previously had time to visit. I was glad I did because I found an excellent restaurant, down near the river, which served the most enormous and spectacular *cuisses de grenouille frites*.

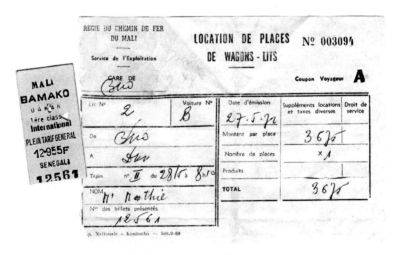

Tickets for more than a thousand miles of 'luxury' travel.

These had been freshly caught in the mighty River Niger as it drifted its muddy way north eastwards a few yards from the restaurant terrace. Served with the feet still on them, they were almost a foot long and one had to be hungry to eat the pile of frogs' legs that arrived on the plate, but they were beautifully cooked and tasted sublime.

In the early morning on 28 May, I presented myself at the station to board the train, which stood waiting surrounded by a milling mob of people so dense that it was almost impossible to move. It is in situations like this that you start to appreciate why Africans carry their loads on their heads. To try and fight my way through the crowd to the carriage, carrying my suitcase in the normal way by my side would have been impossible. Being taller than everyone else in the crowd, I was able, by hoisting it onto my head, to get the case above the level of most obstacles and work my way forward.

It took nearly twenty minutes to find my berth and climb aboard, to discover that I was sharing the compartment with a short and fat Lebanese merchant called Monsieur Picasou. Half of the lower bunk and at least half of the floor was covered in baskets and panniers containing his merchandise. On top of his pile of baggage was an open weave basket of live chickens, with their heads poking out and in the corner, under the window, stood a one-eyed goat.

When he discovered that I was the person who was to share the compartment, Monsieur Picasou obligingly took my suitcase, pulled it in through the window and tossed it onto the top bunk. This left me free to fight my way through the crowd to the end of the carriage and climb aboard. Even then I had to push and squeeze through the press of bodies, for the corridor was choked with other passengers and their luggage as well as all their friends and family members who had come to see them off.

When I finally made it into the compartment and slid the door closed behind me, it was to find my travelling companion hunched over a hissing Primus stove on the floor next to the goat, boiling a pot of water to make mint tea. He welcomed me with a torrent of rapid French which, until I got used to his rather idiosyncratic accent, was difficult to understand. He insisted on my drinking several glasses of his steaming beverage with him. It was cold in the early morning, and the sun was only just above the horizon, so something hot to drink was most welcome although, with the amount of sugar he ladled into each cup, it was more like hot mint syrup than tea.

Just after eight o'clock, the train's horn gave a loud blast which in turn seemed to set off the shrill whistles of attendants hanging out of the doors at the end of each carriage. This was the signal for all those not travelling to disembark and so, with lots of shouted farewells and last-minute messages, the hangers-on gradually descended to the trackside, where they continued their adieus through the open windows of the carriages. Although neither I nor Monsieur Picasou had anyone seeing us off, a crowd of people gathered outside our compartment window to wish us 'Bon voyage' and reach up to shake hands. There were also people trying to sell last-minute provisions and fruit to travellers and the inevitable beggars hoping for a few francs to be cast in their direction.

At ten minutes past eight, the train began, ever so slowly, to move – in the wrong direction. A few moments later and after a number of shuddering jolts, it stopped and began to move in the right direction, gathering speed until it was going at a little more

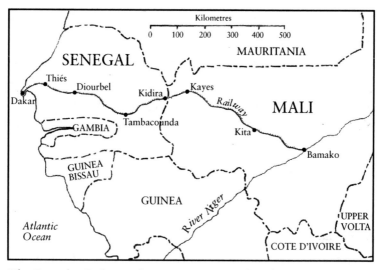

The Bamako-Dakar railway across Senegal and Western Mali.

than fast walking pace. We continued at this speed for several miles while people ran along beside the train, eager to extend the time they shared before losing contact with those who were travelling.

Eventually, well clear of the city, the driver put on speed and the train accelerated to a dizzying thirty miles per hour. We rumbled on westwards at this speed for about an hour, by which time we were past the range of low hills that lies just to the west of the city. The land opened out and we could see scattered villages among the low knobbly trees that speckled the countryside between small patches of cultivation. We saw occasional herds of grazing cattle and the inevitable flocks of goats being tended by small naked boys. From time to time brilliantly coloured birds flitted between the bushes and trees nearest to the track. About two hours into our journey, we passed a group of five giraffes that had obviously crossed the track not long before the train came along.

As the sun climbed higher, the carriage warmed up and I became aware of a smell of fish. Dried slabs of stockfish were a common market commodity in this part of the world, but they have a distinctly salty smell and, anyway, I couldn't see any among Monsieur Picasou's panniers. Perhaps the smell was coming from a neighbouring compartment. There was no obvious source of the smell in our compartment. The goat was slightly rank, but it smelled of goat, not fish. It also had fits of bleating, at which Monsieur Picasou would give it a series of kicks with his smartly shod foot until it subsided into sullen silence, staring at us with its baleful eye.

In the crowded station at Bamako, it had been difficult to get a clear view of much of the train and my attention had been focussed on finding the right carriage and compartment, rather than on the broader perspective. It was only now, when we were under way, that I was able to examine my surroundings properly. From the window I could see most of the train as it went round one of the many curves in the track. The big diesel locomotive looked powerful, if a little dated, and its paintwork, though faded, was reasonably clean and devoid of rust. Whenever the track encountered a slope it emitted great clouds of black smoke from the two fat exhaust stubs on the mid point of its roof. There was a service wagon behind the locomotive that looked drab and functional, with no windows to break up its dull green slab sides. This coach apparently contained the train's kitchen and appeared, by the number of smoke stacks protruding from the rear section of the roof, to be equipped with several wood-fired stoves. This fact was confirmed an hour after we set off when the train halted in the middle of nowhere, beside a stack of cordwood that had been placed beside the track. A hatch in the side of the service wagon opened and two men in chef's attire set about tossing the wood in through the open hatch. After about ten minutes the hatch was closed, the cooks climbed aboard and the train set off again.

The next wagon was the restaurant car. This was, without doubt, the oldest carriage on the train and appeared to have been made well before the end of the nineteenth century. It had engraved glass windows, decorated with ornate urns of flowers and carved curlicues over every window and door set into its rich wooden panelling. It must have been stunning before the African heat made its panels crack and split; but even now its faded glory was spectacular. It even had small crystal chandeliers on intricate ormolu brackets over every dining table and some of the seats retained their original velvet covering, which looked to have once been plush and purple but was now threadbare and faded. The whole carriage was divided into booths either side of the central aisle, with four seats to a booth, two on either side of the table. The dividing partitions had once held glazed panels, but these were now missing and just the ornate frames remained behind the diners' heads.

Behind the restaurant car came the two First Class sleeper coaches. The one Monsieur Picasou and I were in was relatively new, having been made by a Belgian company in 1959, according to the small brass plate affixed to the window frame. It had apparently seen service elsewhere in colonial Africa before being transferred onto the Dakar to Bamako line. It was well appointed with a toilet at each end of the corridor and eight sleeper compartments, each with two bunks. A small metal hand basin was fitted in the corner of each compartment beside the door, but unfortunately these had become ornaments too: the taps were all badly corroded and gave no water; neither were the drains connected to anything, so any liquid that went into the basins would come straight out onto the compartment floor. Monsieur Picasou had adopted our basin as a stand for the small jerrycan in which he kept the water for making his endless supplies of sticky, sweet mint tea.

Behind the sleeper cars came the other passenger carriages, fitted out with wooden seats, but with no lighting and no glass in many of the wide windows. This meant that the Second and Third Class passengers travelled in very draughty conditions with a constant wind across the track buffeting the train and the draught of its passage sending swirling eddies through these carriages. Even so, the passengers seemed a merry bunch and were obviously all glad to have managed to secure a seat of any sort on the train.

Right at the back was the guard's van. This was an oddly shaped, box-like contraption with a platform at the rear where two huge crank-wheels were mounted, one on either side. When turned, these were supposed to apply the emergency brakes if the train's main braking system failed. I had my doubts; they were heavily rusted and looked as if they hadn't been tried in years.

Such an eclectic mix of wagons whose ages spanned three quarters of a century went some way to explaining why, after half a day's travel, the train had yet to exceed the speed of a cantering horse, even when going downhill. This had been demonstrated when, just before the First Class passengers were called for lunch, the train was speeding downhill – speeding being a relative term – and we saw a small group of zebra running along parallel to the track and going faster than the train!

Besides going slowly, the train also made many stops. The fact that it proudly bore the title of The Bamako to Dakar Express was no reason for it not to stop from time to time. In fact, we stopped nineteen times before midday and, at those trackside villages where the driver could not justify stopping, he slowed to walking pace. This was so villagers could come and sell fruit, fresh cashew nuts and other items to the passengers. Vendors carried trays of food on their heads and the passengers reached out of the window and selected what they wanted. Then followed the usual haggling before money was passed and the seller moved on. It was a noisy, joyous process and everyone joined in with good humour and courtesy. I also saw other goods, including baskets of chickens, being passed out of the windows to people who were obviously waiting for them. Never mind express, this train was a mobile market.

Having booked a ticket that included meals, I rather expected lunch to be served in the middle of the day. In this I was to be sadly disappointed. Monsieur Picasou told me that only an evening meal was ever served on the first day of the trip, despite what the booking clerk may have told me. Lunch would be served tomorrow, because we would be in Dakar before evening. All the regular passengers knew this and had come prepared. I could buy some food from one of the trackside vendors, next time we passed through a village, or he could sell me some bread and tinned fish from his merchandise panniers. The smell of fish that had pervaded the compartment all morning was now quite strong and it put me off. I declined his offer as gracefully as I could and made my way forwards along the train.

The restaurant car was largely empty, with just a few seats occupied by passengers who had brought their own food and were taking advantage of the space to spread it out on the tables. Before long we came to another village and the train once more slowed to walking pace. The windows in the restaurant car had already been lowered and it was easy to lean out and buy food. I bought a pawpaw and some tomatoes together with some stale, dusty bread and a small tin of tomato paste for the princely sum of 250 FM (about twenty pence). One of the other passengers, overhearing the price I paid, came and looked at my purchases and told me that I had paid too much. On inspecting the bread more closely, I was inclined to agree. It would be inedible as bread, but might be all right as toast.

I went forward to the kitchen wagon to see if they had a stove burning on which I could toast my bread. An obliging cook looked at it in dismay and said he could have sold me fresh bread. He threw my loaf into the firebox of his stove and handed me a slightly less stale, but much cleaner one from his store. I used one of his knives to split it in half and laid the two pieces on top of the hot iron stove. It only took a few moments to toast. While it was browning, I cranked open my diminutive tin of tomato paste with a borrowed opener and smeared the contents over the two slices of toast before thanking the cook and returning to the restaurant car. My pawpaw and tomatoes were on the table where I had left them.

After my meal I sat for a while, chatting with some of the other passengers and heard wild tales about the train breaking down in the middle of nowhere and having to wait more than a week before anyone from the railway came along. This was apparently because they only had this one train and no other serviceable locomotives, so any other traffic depended on a hand-propelled cart that was capable of taking only three people at little more than walking speed. They were good company and at least the carriage did not smell of fish. Eventually a steward asked us to leave as they had to prepare the restaurant car for the evening meal. I wondered what the preparations involved as I wandered back to my compartment.

As I opened the door, the goat bleated and Monsieur Picasou's leg shot out in a savage kick. "You shouldn't be so cruel," I said.

He just shrugged. "It is a useless animal. It gives no milk," he explained. But he stopped kicking it.

I climbed onto my bunk and lay watching the countryside drift past as the train crawled westwards. It seemed to be keeping up a slightly better average speed now and there were no trackside villages, so fewer stops. The countryside had also changed again and we had entered a region of rocky outcrops and sparser vegetation. Earlier we had been through a well-wooded region with lots of small hillocks scattered across the landscape. We had stopped briefly at one small town, which I think must have been Kita. Some of its houses had been built on stilts. It was strangely attractive and very interesting as I saw no river there, or evidence that the place flooded, but nobody that I asked could explain why the houses were built this way.

In this new region, the trees were more scattered and, except for the ubiquitous mango trees and occasional baobabs, they were slightly smaller, and not as lush as they had been in the countryside we had left behind. There was more thorn scrub and large patches of naked red earth, with fewer and smaller cultivated plots. The few houses that we saw near the track looked different too. Some had fragile walls made of rough sticks with only light thatched roofs, but more and more commonly the buildings were like mud-walled boxes with flat or slightly domed mud roofs. These houses were enclosed in compounds surrounded by shoulder-high mud walls. None of the buildings were painted, so they blended unobtrusively into the stark red landscape.

Three times during that long, hot afternoon, my travelling companion lit his little stove and tried to ply me with tea. Not wanting to appear rude by constantly refusing, I explained that I was unable to manage very sweet things and his tea was loaded with sugar. "*Alors, sans sucre, pas de problème,*" he immediately offered. I was unable to refuse again.

It tasted indescribably disgusting – what was in it heaven only knows – but after making so much fuss, I felt obliged to swallow it. I sipped slowly, pretending to savour it and hoping he would let me off with just one glass, but I had obviously under-estimated him. He took the slowness of my consumption as a sign that I had really enjoyed it and insisted on refilling my glass, against all protests, the minute I had drained it. Fortunately he then decided to go along the corridor to use the toilet, so I was able to throw the second glassful out of the window and pretend to have dozed off when he came back.

At sunset, a steward, freshly washed and smartly attired in a pressed uniform, progressed down the corridor ringing a bicycle bell on a stick and warning the passengers who had booked that the evening meal would be served at seven o'clock. I was hungry and climbed down from my bunk. Monsieur Picasou said he would prefer to skip supper as it was bound to be foul.

"What do you mean?" I asked.

"I make this journey five times every year and the food has always been *dégoûtant* – disgusting," he said. He had brought his own provisions and supplemented that with fruit bought from a trackside vendor in a village we had passed through. I noticed he didn't offer to share his food, nor try to sell me any, so I joined the other passengers who were emerging from their compartments and made my way forward along the train.

In the restaurant car, another steward showed me to a seat at the left hand table in the booth at the front of the coach. My dining companions were already seated. There was a Malian soldier, going to join a unit stationed at Kayes, up towards the Senegalese frontier, a small Senegalese woman with huge, gig-lamp spectacles and a very large, pale skinned man in a grubby *djellabia*. He was most affable and welcomed me warmly as I sat down opposite him. His face wore a permanent grin marred by the absence of two of his front teeth and the fact that all the rest were stained bright red from chewing *kola* nuts.

A waiter carrying two huge steaming bowls of food appeared next to our table. In contrast to the smart, uniformed stewards who had summoned diners and shown us to our tables, this was a scruffy urchin in ragged, grubby, khaki shorts and a torn string vest, badly in need of a wash. He dumped one bowl in front of the soldier and the other in front of the Senegalese woman, before disappearing through the door towards the kitchen. He returned a few moments later with two more bowls of food, dumping one before me and giving the other to the grinning man opposite.

When I had told the steward I was coming to eat, he had asked me to choose my meal from the menu, so that the cooks would know how much of each dish to prepare. The food on offer had been a choice of couscous, couscous or couscous. I chose couscous and wondered if this had been wise. The steaming bowl in front of me did indeed contain couscous, a huge pile of it in fact, over which had been poured a slightly oily looking sauce with a few bits of unidentifiable vegetable and what might once have been meat in it. The couscous was light and fluffy, but everything else had been boiled to oblivion and turned to mush at the touch of a spoon, which was the only cutlery provided.

The other diners all tucked in enthusiastically, so I took a tentative spoonful and was surprised by how good it tasted. This may, of course, have been because apart from one small loaf of toasted bread smeared with tomato paste and two slightly unripe tomatoes, I had eaten nothing for fifteen hours and my stomach was wondering if my throat had been cut. On the other hand, all the other diners couldn't have been that badly wrong when none of them looked ill-fed.

My next spoonful disclosed a small piece of meat attached to a lump of fat. Before I could empty my spoon and pick it up, the big man opposite reached over and fished it out of my bowl, dropping it in his own.

"You don't want to eat all that fat," he told me, replacing the morsel with another from his own bowl. "This is far better. You can crack the bone and eat the marrow."

The lump he dropped back into my bowl consisted of a large bit of bone with minute scraps of meat still attached. I didn't know what to say and looked at the other two diners, in the hope that their reactions might give me some guidance. They didn't. They were both watching me to see what I would do. Only the soldier reacted, leaning towards me and whispering: "He must like you!"

"That is so thoughtful of you," I told the fat man, "but I am required to eat fat. Look how skinny I am; and my teeth are not good enough to crack bones." I patted my pulled-in stomach as I reached across and recovered my bit of meat, dropping the bone back in his bowl in the process. I hastily put the fatty meat in my mouth and started chewing and for the second time that day was revolted by a taste. It was worse than Monsieur Picasou's mint tea. In fact, it was so bad that it made me splutter so I put my hand up to cover my mouth, waving with the other hand towards the jug of water that the waiter had placed on the table.

While the fat man's attention was distracted, pouring me some water, I managed to palm the disgusting morsel and put my hand down on the table next to the open window. I kept chewing – on nothing – for appearances sake, swallowing grandly as I accepted the glass of water. Drinking this thirstily, I slid my hand slightly to the side and released the offending gristle into the African night.

As I dug my spoon once more into my bowl of couscous, the fat man's eyes watched keenly in case some other scrap might appear that he thought would be better in his bowl than in mine. I moved the hand that was holding the water glass so that it impeded his view and carried on eating hungrily. He didn't seem to be put off by this and before long started chatting amiably to the other two travellers who shared our table.

We all stayed in the restaurant car for about an hour after the meal was over, until the lights suddenly failed and we were plunged into darkness. It was only then that I thought about the sparkling chandelier above my head and the cascade of bright light it had shed over our table. Despite the rather diverse mix of passengers, all attired so differently, the restaurant car had had an air of faded opulence that degenerated in the darkness to become nothing more than a cramped, rattling box, swaying as the train dragged itself along through the hot dry night.

The sleeping car steward had been along and made up our bunks by the time I returned to the compartment. As I climbed up into the top bunk, Monsieur Picasou told me that we would arrive at Kayes just after dawn the next morning. "I am leaving the train there," he said. "It is my home and also my trading base."

He offered me another cup of his mint tea before we retired, but I declined, saying I had eaten too much couscous and could not manage anything else. He mumbled on for a few minutes about how disgusting the food must have been, it always was, and eventually he fell silent. I lay on my bunk, enjoying the soft breeze coming through the open window and watching the countryside slide past, bathed in moonlight.

During the night, the train stopped again at another town. The crew took the opportunity to stock up on cordwood in the kitchen car and to replenish all the train's water tanks. This time there were no trackside vendors and the halt lasted only about ten minutes. We were in hilly country now and the land looked more interesting. I was sorry it was not daylight, but at least the moonlight allowed me to see a little of what rolled past.

On we trundled through the night. I learned later that we stopped twice more, but I must have slept through on both occasions for it was only Monsieur Picasou's movement, as he prepared to leave the train, that woke me just before six the next morning. He had his primus stove going of course and was determined that I should share a farewell brew of mint tea with him. This made, he piled most of the panniers that had so far occupied the majority of the floor space onto his bunk, leaving only a small corner on which to sit.

As the sky lightened, the train slowed. Buildings appeared more frequently near the track. Suddenly the view was full of trackside junk, mainly the skeletons of wrecked vehicles and old railway wagons. A few moments later, we reached Kayes station and the train squealed to a halt. It was engulfed in seconds by an exuberant tide of technicolour humanity, some in search of arriving passengers, others waiting to join the train and numerous vendors hawking their wares to passengers who were hanging out of the windows and adding to the cacophony.

Monsieur Picasou's family was waiting to meet him and he began passing his bundles, baskets and panniers out through the open window. There were dozens of items and they made a huge pile beside the track. At last the Primus stove was passed out to a pair of waiting hands; all that remained was Monsieur Picasou and the goat, or so I thought. The smell of fish was still with us, and it smelled even stronger now. It was only then that I discovered its origin.

My little fat travelling companion grabbed hold of the edge of his bunk and heaved it upwards to reveal a large zinc-lined coffer beneath. In this were five enormous fish, three looking like Niger perch, and two huge catfish. They had been packed in ice when they were put into the coffer, but that had all melted some time the previous morning and the resulting water dribbled away though a small drainage hole in the floor to scatter itself along the track.

Monsieur Picasou dragged the top sheet from his bunk and wrapped it round the two catfish before heaving them out through the window. The other three fish were similarly wrapped in the rest of his bedding and passed out the same way. Then he turned to me and I thought it was to say farewell, but no, he wanted me to buy his goat.

I didn't know what to say. I had no immediate use for a goat, didn't really want one, particularly a monocular beast that, as he had told me, gave no milk. But when a deal is offered in Africa, it is rude not to play the game, at least for a moment or two. He was a good and determined salesman and not at all put off by my lack of need for a goat. A few minutes later, when the train's horn blasted to warn of its imminent departure, I found myself 1,000 francs poorer and the confused owner of a dry one-eyed goat.

Working out the exchange rate later, I realised this animal had cost me the grand sum of eighty-three pence.

No new passenger took Monsieur Picasou's berth and as the train gathered speed and headed towards the Senegalese frontier, I pondered the question of what was I going to do with the goat when we reached Dakar. I was booked into the Hotel Oceanic, but the management don't normally expect people, especially Europeans, to arrive with their livestock at heel. I was also scheduled to attend a number of meetings in ministries and other government offices before going off to tour a series of water development projects in the hinterland. I couldn't very well take the goat with me.

In the end, that is precisely what I did.

AFTER KAYES, THE TRAIN travelled at a speed more appropriate for an international express and it was not long before we stopped at the customs post on the Malian side of the bridge over the Senegal River. The formalities did not take long and involved a uniformed official walking the length of the train saying hello to everyone. I saw him check only one person's papers. When he reached the guard's van, he skipped down to the track, the guard waved his flag and the train rolled forward, across the bridge and stopped at the Senegalese post on the other side.

Another uniformed official came down the train. He glanced at many of the offered passports but his examination was only superficial. He too climbed down to the track when he reached the guard's van, shook hands with the guard and waved the train onwards.

The countryside became less broken soon after we crossed the border, undulating with broad open views over sandy semi-desert, numerous baobab trees and occasional scattered settlements breaking up the monotony. Surprisingly, until we reached Diourbel, none of the settlements were close to the railway track, but there were intermittent clusters of people who had foregathered at regular spots, typically near the top of each gradient, to try and sell produce to the train's passengers.

After another line of low hills, the track entered an area with more cultivation. Fields of millet and sugar cane rippled in the breeze like waves on a sandy green ocean. Fewer trees grew, with just one or two tall acacias standing out like beacons in the otherwise empty landscape. Many had what appeared to be rolls of grass matting stuffed high in their branches and I wondered what strange taboo they embodied. This idea was later corrected by my fat dining companion, who informed me that they were a traditional form of beehive peculiar to the region.

Lunch was served at midday on this second day of the journey and I found myself again sharing the table with two of my companions from the previous evening. The fat man was again most affable and keen to practice his rather bad French on me. The Senegalese woman, who had previously been silent, was chatty this time. I soon discovered that her reticence had been because the soldier, who had left the train at Kayes, was a friend of her brother and had once made advances but had been refused by her father.

The choice of food for lunch was ragout, ragout or ragout, with couscous. On the fat man's recommendation, I chose ragout and couscous and received broad smiles from the steward to confirm the wisdom of my choice. The meal was, unsurprisingly, virtually the same as the night before. The leftover vegetables from that meal had dissolved or been mashed into a pulp that became the new sauce to which a few new bits had been added. The meat component had been replaced by fish and I immediately wondered if Monsieur Picasou had sold some of his smelly cargo to the kitchen crew. The fish was in big lumps and, to my surprise, had no bones in it. On balance it turned out to be one of the better meals that I have had while on the move in West Africa.

The train stopped only twice as we crossed the country and it was noticeable that it now travelled at a much greater and more consistent speed. "This is because our people maintain the track better," the Senegalese woman told me. "There is less risk of derailment by going too fast." The line was not, she claimed, so well maintained in Mali.

The train's crew had changed at the frontier and were now more smartly dressed and businesslike than the Malian crew, so this explanation had a ring of truth about it.

By early afternoon the countryside had changed again. Much more of the land was under cultivation and we passed occasional herds of healthy looking hump-backed cattle. Millet gave way to maize as the principal crop and near many of the houses were fields of cotton and neat vegetable patches. This area was also more populated; children outside most of the houses interrupted their games to wave at the train. I looked along the outside of the train and saw many arms waving back.

At about half past three, we entered the beginnings of the urban sprawl that surrounds every big city in Africa. The trackside was again littered with the remains of wrecked vehicles, including some huge lorries that must have been used to haul rock and dirt to make some of the new embankments on which the line had been laid about thirty years ago. Behind this metal jungle was the most enormous *bidonville* slum, its occupants busy along the trackside selling all manner of goods and produce, trying to scrape a living out of the passing rail traffic while using the open space the line provided as a highway for pedestrians and bicycles.

For nearly half an hour, the train rolled through this slum at a speed slightly in excess of a trot, and its rampant poverty shouted at us in the luxury of our train carriages. We crossed several good tarmac roads before the shanties suddenly vanished from view. In their place appeared a patch of open farmland with neat houses made of concrete blocks, surrounded by vegetable gardens and dotted with numerous fat baobab and tall kapok trees. A few minutes later, we rolled into the city and the buildings became more substantial. The train entered the terminus and came to a smooth hissing stop with only a slight squeal from the brakes.

Dakar station had five tracks leading out of it, but only one was usable as the others were missing sleepers and sections of rail. The tracks had been laid in a bygone age when the colonial power had dreams of building a rail network to compare with that of metropolitan France. They built an imposing terminus with a wide vaulted roof and an ornate facade that is still surprisingly elegant today. Sadly, apart from a line up the coast to Saint Louis and the line to Bamako, little came of those ambitious plans; two world wars and years of minimal economic development meant the expenditure could not be justified, so the building stopped. The natural resources of the hinterland which, had they been efficiently exploited, might have generated the necessary cash, had proved to be insufficient to justify the investment because Senegal is far from mineral rich and its agriculture remains too near the subsistence level to be of major economic value. Similarly, Mali's only mineral resource, the Taoudéni salt mine, is situated so far north in an inaccessible part of the Sahara that it offered no

The elegant façade of Dakar's imposing railway terminus, legacy of a bygone era.

trade for the railway either. Its exploitation has always been uneconomical for anything but camel caravans, so the rail network was never built.

Once more there were crowds around the train, but less dense here as the Senegalese staff were effective at blocking access to the platforms to those who came to meet the train. As a result, disembarkation was less frenetic and I found it fairly easy to lower my suitcase from the window to the ground, to take hold of the string around my goat's neck and lead her along the corridor to the carriage door. I found my bag still where I had dropped it and hoisted it onto my head before heading for the exit with my goat.

Nobody took any notice of me or the goat, but then many of the passengers carried baggage on their heads and had baskets of chickens among their luggage, so it probably didn't look too incongruous. I did, however, encounter a problem outside when I tried to get a taxi to take me to my hotel. There were half a dozen taxis waiting for fares, but they all balked at taking the goat. A basket of chickens was, apparently, acceptable, but not my goat.

After trying all the waiting cabs, none of which was getting much trade from the other arrivals, I declared loudly that I would walk to my hotel and tell everyone there, when I arrived, how unhelpful the Dakar taxi drivers were. It didn't occur to me until later that it was probably the stink of fish that still hung around me like some evil miasma, rather than the goat, that made the taxi drivers disinclined to accept my fare.

With this declaration, I set off down the road, not entirely sure where I was going, but leading my goat by its string and with my suitcase balanced on my head. I had only gone a hundred yards before one of the taxis pulled up just ahead of me and the driver leapt out to try and get me into his cab. We then started a vigorous discussion about the cost of the proposed journey. It should have been a standard 300 CFA francs, but, in view of the goat, and to keep his pride intact, he insisted that I pay at least 750. We dickered for a few minutes until one of the other taxis passed us, honking his horn and shouting from his window. Then he caved in and we settled on 450 CFA. This translated to about seventy pence. Once I was installed in the back of the taxi, the driver was actually helpful and happy to answer my questions about the city. I told him that I had business in town for four days and would then be departing for the countryside and asked if he would like some regular fares. Since he evidently knew the city very well, it seemed a good idea to hire him as my driver. We settled on a price of 4,000 CFA. When we reached my hotel, I tore four 1,000 CFA franc notes in half, giving him one half of each and keeping the other bits. I promised that at the end of each day I would replace one of the halves with a brand new banknote and that I would also buy his lunch. I paid my fare from the station and went inside confident that he would turn up the next day.

The hotel manager was a fat little mulatto whose nose wrinkled when he saw that I had brought a goat with me. We argued about it for a while, but he finally agreed that I could tie it up in the garden. His gardener's son could bring me some fodder for it and I would be well advised to hire the boy to ensure that the goat did not eat his flowers. This seemed like a good idea, so I hired the boy for 200 CFA a day and gave him an extra fifty to buy the fodder. He seemed delighted. The hotel manager told me I had overpaid the boy. As he did so, he kept stepping away from me and sniffing. This was when I finally realised that it was the smell of fish that was putting everyone off. Our business concluded and with my goat's needs attended to, I went to my room for a shower, keen to get the smell of fish out of my hair and clothes at long last.

The Hotel Oceanic was considered to be one of the better small hotels in Dakar. When I finally left, sixteen days later, my bill, which was written on a scrappy bit of squared paper, torn out of a school exercise book, came to 12,800 CFA. This was £20.32 for the whole period, or £1.27 per day. This sum included breakfast, evening meals, laundry and lodging for my goat. I could now see why the manager thought I had overpaid my goat boy.

SINCE I MADE THAT TRIP things have changed a lot. For several years, no trains at all ran from Bamako to Dakar because both the track and the trains were unfit for use. Then a Canadian company bought an interest and still operates the railway today.

One train per week now runs in each direction – if you are lucky. The journey now takes at least forty-four hours, usually a

The Bop Centre, Dakar: part eye clinic, part youth club.

lot more, and may run ten or more hours late on a good trip. The fare has increased too and it now costs 52,000 CFA for the same trip that I made, which, at the current exchange rate, makes the journey cost £54.73.

Some things, however, do get better with time. The railway company now sells cold beer on the train. You can also get three good meals a day while travelling, but not in the price of the ticket, something they don't tell you when you book.

As for the one-eyed goat, it didn't end up in the pot as you might have expected, although it did feed many mouths. Next door to the eye clinic I visited in the north of the city was a small children's centre, run by the organisation that had started the eye clinic, to care for children while they were patients. It had evolved into a long-term home for many of the children, and being run on a shoe string meant food was always a problem.

I realised that once the goat had produced a kid, it would begin giving milk again, so I asked the centre if they would like to give it a home. Before handing it over, I arranged an encounter with a billy goat and five months later a female kid was born. The one-eyed goat gave milk which, within a few weeks, was being shared with the children.

The head of the eye clinic, Dr Adrien, had taken a keen interest when I told him how I had come to own the goat. The following year when I visited he showed me the goat, which now had two kids at heel and was milking well. It also had two working eyes. Dr Adrien, wanting to introduce a new treatment to his clinic, had trialled the procedure successfully on the goat and restored its full binocular vision.

3 ~ The poetic president

I FELT SLIGHTLY OUT OF PLACE mingling with the diplomatic crowd in Senegal until I bumped into the minister responsible for the country's water resources. He was as uncomfortable as I was, having only recently been appointed to his post and not in the habit of attending state banquets. Not that I was either, but an official invitation had arrived from the President's office requesting my presence at this celebration of Senegal's contribution to the West African Economic Union. I telephoned to see if there had been some mistake, but was assured that there had been none and I was expected.

The event started with a cocktail party at which the hundred and fifty guests were able to mingle and exchange diplomatic courtesies before President Léopold Senghor put in his appearance. He was no longer a young man and liked to limit the amount of time he was obliged to spend on such functions, preferring instead, so it was said, to sit in his study and write poetry – for which he had achieved international recognition – when he wasn't busy reading state papers.

The minister looked with distaste at the insipid cocktail he had been handed and asked if I might prefer to drink beer. He knew how to get some if I would care to accompany him. His suggestion was most welcome because the cocktails were every bit as tasteless as they appeared.

It was as we were working our way across the crowded room, like two conspiratorial schoolboys, that we had the misfortune to come face to face with Her Britannic Majesty's representative. Our paths had not previously crossed but I had been warned that this man had a propensity to be abrasive with those he considered inferior. That covered just about everyone.

"Aha! Mathie," he announced. His accent betrayed him as originating somewhere in the Rhondda valley. It sounded misplaced in Africa. "I thought I caught sight of a kilt among this otherwise properly dressed gathering and wondered if it was you." He glanced at the minister before continuing his assault. "This is supposed to be for special guests of the President and his government, not for roughs. So what the devil are you doing here? An' who's this chappie, anyway?" He jerked his thumb towards the minister, as though thumbing a lift.

"Good evening, Excellency," I said. I was certain he would have studied the guest list carefully and knew perfectly well it was me. Still, his manner took me aback slightly although I recognised he couldn't help either being Welsh or of diminutive stature. Most of the British diplomats I had encountered around that time were simpering and obsequious; he was abrupt and pompous. "May I introduce Minister Antoine Aloumye, Excellency? His ministry oversees many of our development projects across the country."

The ambassador had not risen to his position without picking up the skills of his trade. His face gave nothing away. His manner, however, as he shook the minister's hand, underwent an instant about face and he transformed into the suave groveller that I had expected him to be.

"How nice to meet you, ambassador," the minister said, calmly ignoring the insult. "You must make an appointment and come round to my ministry some time so that we can review the projects your government is assisting with. Now, if you will excuse me, I was taking Monsieur Mathie to introduce him to one of my colleagues." He took my elbow and steered me away quickly. I went willingly, leaving the bemused *chargé d'affaires* standing with nobody to talk to.

We found our beer and secluded ourselves in a corner to chat until dinner was announced. The minister asked what all that had been about. "Nothing much," I replied. "Just another one of the types our government insists on employing as diplomats showing what a prat he can be."

SOON AFTERWARDS WE parted as we were seated at different ends of the room during the banquet. I had looked at the seating plan on arrival and noticed that the minister was seated opposite the Her Majesty's man. Having now encountered him, I wondered who was going to enjoy the event least. I liked this minister and hoped those on either side of him would be good company. When I found my own place it was to discover that I was seated next to two people I already knew, for I had met them both some months previously, one just before and the other during my first visit to Senegal.

One was Ousmane Baba Kamaru, a cousin of Mali's president. He had invited me to dinner in Bamako and had been instrumental in turning my rather crazy idea of an earthwork dam into a full blown development programme, with his cousin's help.

He was an elegant man, dressed in an expensive robe of white brocade.

The man on my other side was a charming Italian Cardinal, the Papal Legate to Senegal and its neighbouring states. He lived, and had his office, in a large seafront villa, just outside the city, on the northern side of the isthmus and had once told me he was in no hurry to return to Rome. The first time I had met him I was delivering a letter from one of the Catholic missionaries I knew in Mali. The Cardinal was always interested in what was going on in the interior and obviously had very good sources of information, so he invited me to drink wine with him on his terrace overlooking the Atlantic while he enquired about where I had been and whom I had met. We enjoyed lively and entertaining discussions, both then and now.

Ousmane Baba was being monopolised by the person on his other side, so unfortunately I had less time to talk to him than I would have liked. It was rare to have this sort of access to those in power and I was aware that he had influence far beyond that which he had already deployed to assist me. I wanted to know a lot more about this man, quite apart from the fact that I found his company enjoyable. Even so, the Cardinal was excellent company and a fluent conversationalist on many interesting topics.

The dinner was superb, although for some reason these four words were all I recorded in my notebook about the meal and I have no recollection of what we ate. I do remember that it was served with excellent French wines that had supposedly been chosen by the President himself. He had once served as the Minister of Finance in the metropolitan French government in Paris and had acquired considerable knowledge on the subject. He was also a member of the Academie Française, that venerable body which oversees the French language and culture, maintaining its purity, among other things. At this time he was the only 'foreigner' ever to have held such an august position.

After dinner we had to sit through the inevitable speeches. A couple were short, politically loaded diatribes from members of the government on Senegal's importance to the region. They were followed by an excellent speech on the successes of West African unity that was delivered by the president of Côte d'Ivoire, Félix Houphouet-Boigny. He too had once served as a French metropolitan minister. It looked as if the speeches were going to go on for hours, but our host evidently had other ideas.

PRESIDENT SENGHOR ROSE to his feet, thanked the guests for coming and uttered a few beautifully crafted words to celebrate his country's contribution to the economic union. We were expecting another long eulogy about the noble attributes of Senegal and all its wonderful achievements in the last ten years. Not so: he stopped the speech after only two minutes, laid down his notes and announced that he would read us some of his poetry.

For the next half hour he held the whole audience spellbound with his verses. Even those who spoke French poorly must have been impressed by the beauty of his language, the elegance of his expression and the moods created by his poetry. At last he sat down and his audience rose to their feet in applause, which lasted for a full ten minutes.

When the applause began to slacken, the President again rose to his feet and headed towards the door. This was the signal that the banquet was over and we should now proceed once more to the anteroom, where the President would receive and greet all his guests individually before we went home. He stationed himself just beyond the doorway, together with a line of his most distinguished guests, to whom he was introducing selected other guests as they came out. An equerry stood next to the President and asked each person's name as they reached the front of the queue. This was then whispered to the President so that he could greet the guest by name and exchange a few words before passing them on.

As my turn came, I gave my name, the equerry whispered and the President shook my hand, saying: "I hear the fishing villages along the lower Senegal River now have clean drinking water thanks to you, Monsieur Mathie." I was most impressed by how well he had been briefed.

"The people themselves, and your officials, have done all the hard work, Excellency. I have merely provided some knowledge, some funding and been a small catalyst," I replied.

"Senegal is grateful, nonetheless," he said. "I hope you have enjoyed our small celebration?"

"Very much, Excellency," I replied. "I particularly liked your poem about the beehives."

"Ah, that one. Thank you. I wrote it originally in Ouolof, some years ago, and I had to translate it. It lost a little in translation, but still has an element of traditional romance about it. I wonder if the modern hives, that are now being introduced, will ever evoke such feelings?" He looked slightly wistful. "Let me introduce you to my good friend from Mali, President Traoré." He handed me on to the man standing on his left, who was grinning broadly.

"We are old friends," said Moussa Traoré, as indeed we had met before. I told him that I had again enjoyed his cousin's company at dinner and he seemed amused. "I'll have to exile him to the salt mines and put a stop to these clandestine meetings you keep having, before things go too far," he laughed. "Now let me introduce you to my good friend President Eyadema of Togo. He has similar problems to those on the Senegal River and could use your help. Come and see me next time you are in Bamako." He handed me on smoothly to the man on his left.

I was surprised to discover the extent to which President Etienne Eyadema was already aware of the project on the Senegal River, and wondered how and why that had come about. He asked if I had written a report on the scheme and whether it would be infringing anyone's confidentiality if he asked for a copy. I promised to ask the minister's permission and to send him one, before leaving him and moving out into the room to join the other guests.

As I looked back, I saw the little Welshman reach the receiving line. President Senghor shook his hand, said a couple of words and then turned his attention to the next guest without handing him on to any of the other distinguished men in the line-up. Apparently unaware of the snub, the ambassador progressed into the room like a frigate under full sail.

I turned away in search of someone else to talk to and found myself next to Dr Adrien and his wife, a Senegalese couple who ran a small eye clinic at Bop, in the northern part of the city. This was a man I was due to visit later in the week, so the meeting was fortuitous and I would gladly have discussed working matters with him until it was time to leave. His wife, however, had other ideas and was particularly keen to talk about her President's poetry, of which she was a dedicated *aficionado*.

Eventually we all left and I returned to my hotel, where I was awake for most of the night with severe indigestion. Two days later following a successful meeting with the doctor in Bop, I started the long trek back to Lomé, in Togo, where I was temporarily based.

4 ~ The sorcerer's spells

WHEN I FIRST ARRIVED IN Lomé, I lived down in the lower part of the city, no more than two hundred metres from the sea. Across the road from my house was a narrow strip of sandy ground, backed by a cactus hedge. This hedge was, in fact, the Ghana border.

The men who lived in the low buildings just beyond the hedge emerged every morning to manufacture concrete blocks. They did this on the sandy strip between the hedge and the road, on the Togolese side of the border. Regular patrols of Ghanaian and Togolese frontier guards strolled up and down the strip, chatting to everyone, seemingly very relaxed and friendly. Although there was an official road crossing point down at the sea front, the local people appeared to wander back and forth across the border with impunity.

The building I occupied had my office on the ground floor, with a large apartment above and a broad balcony looking out over the border road. The building was set back in a compound, surrounded by a five foot high block wall, whose lattice-like blocks had been made by the Ghanaian men across the road.

The frontier block works in Lomé: the border between Togo and Ghana was a cactus hedge.

My neighbour on the seaward side was Antoine, the Togolese manager of the Air Afrique office in the city. The house on the other side belonged to the UN and was occupied by a pair of bachelors: Mickal, a young Dutchman, who worked for UNICEF and a Belgian forester called Lucien, who managed a number of UN programmes.

Antoine's house had a well-established garden that made both my house and the UN house look bare and shabby. The UN team had only recently taken possession of their property and workmen had not finished painting it until the week before I arrived. Now the occupants were giving their attention to the garden.

Mickal, being Dutch and from a tulip growing family, was something of a specialist in bulbs, both European and tropical, so he sought out all sorts of interesting plants to fill their garden. Each time Lucien returned from a trip up-country to visit his forestry projects, he brought back a selection of interesting young trees and colourful shrubs. Finding that I was keen to get a garden growing, the two of them were more than willing to share these with me and to help get things growing in my plot. The only thing that didn't want to grow was grass and, defying all our efforts to plant seed and lay turf, my lawn remained bare for many months, while others along the road were lush and green.

One day Lucien arrived smiling and excited. He had brought some seeds home from the forest that he thought might interest me. Most of the houses in the road either had solid, painted walls surrounding them, or had well-established hibiscus hedges. Mine had a naked grey lattice of concrete blocks that would have been fiddly to paint and desperately needed covering with some form of vegetation.

Lucien had discovered a creeper that was, he claimed, just what was required and would cover the unsightly wall in no time. He showed me a handful of large, shiny, dark brown seeds about the size of broad beans. He suggested planting one at either end of the wall on each side of the entrance gate. This would put the seeds at least thirty feet apart and I asked if this wasn't perhaps a little sparse if we hoped to cover the wall quickly. I pointed out that these would be a long way apart as there was at least ten metres of wall on either side of the gate.

"Not at all," Lucien assured me, "this vine grows so fast you can see it! In less than a month there will be no more wall." He gave me two of the seeds. I looked at them speculatively and wondered if this was a subtle Belgian joke as I heeled them in where he suggested and poured water over them.

He was right. Within three weeks, the wall was covered by a lush creeper with dark green heart shaped leaves. Each leaf was the size of my spread hand and I have large hands. The stems of the creeper and the backs of its leaves were covered with a coating of fine silver hairs that looked like velvet but made one itch interminably for a week, if one was careless enough to touch them. They also left a rash that took much longer to subside, even under the soothing influence of modern unguents and medicinal creams.

During my second week in Lomé, I hired as a cook a man called Clément Aladaye. He was a smiling chap of about my own age, who came from Nuatja, a small town about a hundred kilometres north of the city. He had learned to cook while working in a number of European residences in the city and claimed to make the best *crème brulée* in Lomé. I liked him immediately and felt that even if he was no good as a cook, he would be a good henchman, fun to have around and I could safely entrust the place to his care when I was away on field trips.

My trust was well rewarded, for he turned out to be an excellent cook, with an interesting repertoire of dishes and his *crème brulée* was everything he claimed. Indeed, he had a reputation for it and, within a couple of weeks of engaging him, no fewer than three attempts to poach him were made by members of the international diplomatic community. To my great relief, Clément did not want to go, despite being offered four times as much as I was paying him by the French Ambassador's wife.

"I don't like the French," he told me, after she had left. "They are so rude and they are all snobs." Later, as I got to know the expatriates in Lomé, I had to agree with him.

Inevitably, Clément and I became friends and he brought his wife and young daughter to meet me one evening. Analou, his wife, came from the same town as Clément, but spoke very little French, although she was quite well educated by Togolese standards. Their daughter, Juliette, was a sweetie; immaculately dressed, with a ready smile and all the charm that little girls of six have the world over. She was just learning to read and write and very proudly showed me how well she could write her own name.

After this first visit, Analou and Juliette would often call at the house during the day, to speak to Clément while they were out doing their own daily chores, and he would accompany them to the market as he bought food for me. It never occurred to me that he might abuse this trust by buying his own food at my expense until one of the wives from the British Embassy assured me that he would. But Clément's accounting was always exact. I was pleased for her to be proved so wrong.

MY FIRST TRIP INTO the hinterland was just over a month after I arrived. Leaving Clément in charge of the house, I headed off on the long, slow road north to Lama Kara, where a major development project was nearing the completion of its first phase. I took with me a young Togolese man from the Ministry of Agriculture, called Ekiéné Gnoketun. He was destined to become the project manager for the second phase and I thought that travelling together for a few days would provide a good opportunity for us to get to know one another. Ekiéné was slightly late at the rendezvous and somehow never quite managed to catch up during the whole three-week trip. This was, however, his only failing and he proved to be very good at his job once the second phase began.

No development project ever goes completely to plan, particularly in West Africa. The Lama Kara project was spread over a wide geographical area and involved three quite different tribal groups, each with its own traditions, attitudes and

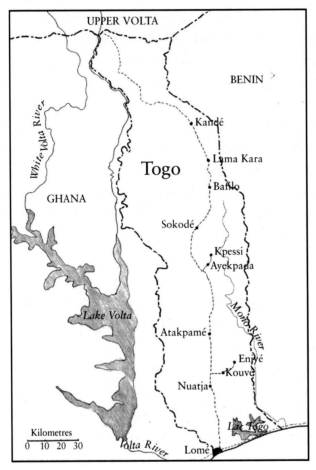

République du Togo.

aspirations. It was, of course, out of these differences that trouble first showed its face, along the unseen border between two of the tribes.

There were age-old disagreements that are regularly raked over by each succeeding generation and the way in which project work was to be shared out was the excuse used by the current generation to revive these differences. During the first eighteen months, there had been at least half a dozen occasions when work had ceased for two or three weeks while long-winded and sometimes acrimonious negotiations had been held to settle things.

Now, as we were getting ready to launch the second phase, disputes flared up again, with one tribe accusing its neighbour of secretly taking more of the cash crops produced by their joint effort and thereby profiting at the expense of their neighbours. What should have been a festive, celebratory event, to mark the successes of Phase One turned into a petty squabbling match with acrimony as thick as the wood smoke from the village cooking fires that permeated the air. This was, unfortunately, further fuelled by the food and drink that had been laid on for a celebratory feast as each group, becoming more and more intoxicated, refused to eat with the others.

At some point, one of the tribes brought their witch-doctor into the action. A drab little man dressed in scruffy clothes decorated with a random collection of animal tails and bracelets of small metal bells, he strutted back and forth between the opposing ranks, declaiming curses and invocations in a sharp staccato voice and aiming them at any individual who attempted to interrupt his tirade.

This had been going on for about ten minutes when a sorcerer from the other tribe entered the arena. This man was much more flamboyantly dressed in a skin kilt with ribbons of monkey fur and a leopard skin cap. He wore bunches of feathers round his upper arms and was waving a long stick festooned with rattling seed pods and loosely attached bones. He too strutted up and down like a gaily plumed bantam cock, spouting curses left and right against members of the opposing tribe as he rattled his stick and waved a horsehair fly whisk for emphasis.

There was nothing anyone could do to stop this business, for anyone who tried to intervene immediately became the target for both sorcerers' curses. It was only after they had been going for about half an hour that they began to slow down, as though they were running out of curses. Not so, they were preparing for a united assault on the project managers who, they alleged, had been thoroughly partisan in the way they had divided up the work and allocated the rewards. Delivering their imprecations alternately, the two witch-doctors began a tirade of very personal abuse against each member of the management team. Ironically this included many of their own tribal elders, for we had been careful to involve them throughout the project.

While I could easily pick up on the mood and emotions of these men, I understood not a word, for it was all delivered very fast in the local dialect. Ekiéné translated some of it for me at the time and recounted a lot more to me later. Most of the curses were quite mild, calling for individuals to suffer periods of painful indigestion, or be plagued by boils for a time commensurate with the degree of injustice they were alleged to have caused. Some called for more draconian punishments, like the death of livestock or the affliction of terrible diseases, while others threatened the well-being of another's crops with the implication that they should fail and leave the man and his family hungry.

I was not, at the time, aware of any curses pointed directly at me, although by association I was quite probably included in the general curses doled out to the project's management team. If so, I could expect my hair to turn red, to get painful corns on my feet, to suffer several days of galloping diarrhoea and for my skin to become blotchy and peel off in sheets. Since my hair had been red until it was bleached by the African sun at the age of four and sunburn and the trots are a daily hazard of living in tropical climes, it didn't seem unreasonable that the witch-doctors' predictions might come true. Unless there was something Ekiéné hadn't translated, I didn't think I had any particular reason to feel unduly threatened by these men. Also, being new to the project, I didn't feel in any way responsible for the alleged injustices and felt it more appropriate to take their words as a warning for the next phase.

After a couple of hours things began to settle down and some semblance of normality emerged. Perhaps it was the food that people didn't want to see going to waste, or maybe the two witch-doctors had finally run out of steam. Eventually, the tribal elders who had been involved with the project from the beginning, started talking to one another like reasonable men and others followed suit. Somebody produced a drum, another a balafon, someone else a reed flute and soon people were dancing and the rest of the event passed off with at least superficial harmony.

For the time being, tribal honour appeared to have been satisfied. The sorcerers' curses slipped from my mind, replaced by more pressing project matters. The next three days were taken up with detailed explanations and negotiations about the next phase which was due to begin imminently.

Phase One of the project had been very successful. The Togolese government now wanted to press ahead, extending things much more rapidly than had originally been planned. They were obviously looking for the prestige that would permit them to brag about the improvements they had brought to the northern rural communities when elections came round next year. Elections are something of a sham in a dictatorship like Togo, but the politicians like to keep up the pretence of democracy and it gave them an opportunity to shout publicly about the merits of their achievements and to bolster their personal popularity.

But this was only one of a multiplicity of factional interests and the divergent views made Ekiéné and I approach things quite cautiously. We knew that some lip service would have to be paid to government demands and Ekiéné was, after all, a civil servant. But he was also a realist. He understood how easily a project could over-extend itself, beyond the possibility of recovery and, since he was to be the project manager, he didn't want either his name or the project tarnished by that sort of debacle.

In preparation for the ongoing phases, which would soon see the establishment of an agricultural school, a project centre the size of a small village had been built. At the moment all the buildings were of the traditional mud brick and thatch construction that typified the villages of the Lama Kara area. Later, when classrooms, laboratories and student accommodation blocks were needed, the new buildings would be large rectangular structures, built of concrete blocks and probably topped with wriggly tin roofs which, despite their unsuitability for this environment, were seen as a status symbol. The rural population of this region loved bright shiny things and a shiny silver roof would be worthy of great admiration. For students to learn under such a roof would enhance the perceived value of their learning enormously.

The huts where Ekiéné and I were accommodated during the negotiations were traditional round huts with conical thatched roofs. The interior walls had been whitewashed and the accommodation, though spartan, was comfortable enough. In truth, we only slept in our huts, spending all the rest of our time out and about around the project's multiple working sites.

The night after the sorcerers' battle, I found myself scratching a lot when I went to bed. I assumed it was mosquitoes and made sure that my net was well tucked in. Even so, by morning I had scratched myself raw; so had Ekiéné. Before going to bed that night I sprayed my hut with Flit and lit a mosquito repellent coil which smouldered away during the night filling the air with a faint aroma of toasted insecticide.

My precautions made not the slightest difference. For a second night, both Ekiéné and I itched and scratched and by morning we had decided that the problem was not mosquitoes, but fleas. We shook out all our bedding and hung it in the sun to try and kill off any infestations. We swept out our huts and made sure that we had fresh sheets to suspend below the roof when evening came to stop anything from falling from the thatch. Again, just before retiring, we sprayed the huts liberally with insecticide and lit mosquito coils.

We were still bitten raw by something and had to seek out a local medicine woman to make a salve from astringent leaves for us to soothe our itching bodies. It all made concentrating on the project negotiations rather difficult and we got some funny looks from most of the elders. It was almost as though they knew something we didn't and I wondered momentarily if fleas had featured in the bounty of curses doled out by the battling witch-doctors.

At one point the negotiations almost broke down when one of the tribal elders seemed to be going back on something that had already been settled. When he tried to introduce yet another retraction into the discussion, I told him off for being unreasonable and inconsistent. He obviously didn't like this, but backed down and, reluctantly, returned to what he had previously

The Great North highway between Bafilo and Lama Kara.

agreed. I watched him carefully from then on, and listened attentively every time he spoke, to make sure that he did not try the same gambit again. I had suspicions about this man because I had seen him several times in deep and clearly private conversation with one of the sorcerers who had performed so dramatically at the celebration.

Eventually we came to the end. The details were all agreed and the tribes expressed themselves satisfied and ready to start work. A chicken was slaughtered and every man dipped his index finger in it and placed his mark on the record. Ekiéné and I packed our bags to make the long journey back to Lomé to complete the last formalities with the Togolese administration. Ekiéné would be back in a couple of weeks to launch the next phase.

On the journey south, we planned to stop at several other projects for brief inspection visits, but first we paused for lunch in Bafilo, a town on the main arterial road about twenty-five kilometres south of Lama Kara. As happens everywhere in Africa, the presence of strangers at the local eatery attracted a crowd of curious onlookers. Most of these were children, but among the few adults was one rather strange looking man with a squint and one blue eye. His hair was in dreadlocks, which was uncommon in Togo at that time, and he wore a number of diagonal bandoliers consisting of bones and strange plant husks on coloured fibre cords, with odd beads, beans and cowrie shells hanging from them. He had what looked like a rusty chain mail collar round his neck.

This strange individual stared at us as we ate, his attention unwavering. Ekiéné was the first to notice his intense interest and called out to ask him what he wanted. The man continued to stare but said nothing. When the restaurant owner brought us drinks, we asked her if she knew who the man was, thinking that he might have been the local madman, who would be well-known and tolerated in the community. She did not know this man and after looking closely at him, offered the opinion that he was some sort of a sorcerer and best left alone.

This suggestion unsettled Ekiéné. He disliked sorcery and after the events of the last few days, he felt threatened by it, so we finished out meal and left as soon as possible. A hundred kilometres further south we turned off the main road and trundled a short distance down the Kpessi road to visit a poultry breeding project at Ayekpada.

The project staff welcomed us warmly and took us on a tour of their establishment, explaining how everything was managed and showing us the way they were training local farmers in poultry husbandry. The centre had been in operation for almost two years and had a lot to show us. We were also able to meet several local farmers who had started keeping poultry after attending training at the centre. Most were now doing quite well and all agreed that they had benefited greatly from their training.

When we came back to our vehicle it was to find an unwelcome surprise. Staring at the vehicle from a range of ten feet was the strange man who had earlier watched us eating. How had he got here when we had left him over a hundred kilometres north? Ekiéné was really rattled to see him and strode over to demand an explanation. The man stared as if looking straight through him and said nothing.

We made a hurried farewell to the project manager, climbed into the Land Rover and left in a cloud of yellow dust.

A hundred and fifty kilometres further south we turned off the main road again and headed off to the east. There was a forestry project that Ekiéné wanted to visit at a place called Eniyé, just beyond Kouvé. I was keen to see it myself for it was one of the schemes that my neighbour Lucien was working on and it would be interesting to see, first hand, the work he was doing. Ekiéné needed to discuss the next year's funding and had arranged for us to stay overnight.

The foresters gave us a good tour of their plantation and showed us the nursery where they were breeding some new fast growing hardwood trees using seed that had been brought in from Gabon. They had also started a small rubber plantation but the trees were still several years away from producing any latex. After supper, they sat down with Ekiéné to hold their conference while I wrote up some more notes about our visit to Lama Kara. It was close to midnight when we finally retired to sleep.

In the morning when we woke, Ekiéné was first up and he headed out into the dappled sunshine. He was back moments later, agitated, shaking and almost incoherent, pointing outside.

His face was grey and it was clear that he had had a significant shock. I went out to see what it was, expecting to find that the tyres had been stolen from our Land Rover or something equally silly and was completely unprepared for the sight that met my eyes. There, standing on one foot, staring at the Land Rover, was the strange man we had seen twice the previous day.

I went over and spoke to him, but he ignored me. I took hold of his arm and shook it, asking again who he was and what he wanted with us. Maybe he did not speak French, but he gave no indication that he had even heard me. When I shook his arm again he turned and looked at me, his face devoid of all recognition or expression, his eyes empty as if he was sightless, and still he said nothing. When I let go of his arm he returned his focus to the Land Rover and I felt the first frisson of unease.

I walked round the vehicle, looking at it carefully, but could see nothing amiss. The doors were still locked and the tyres were not flat. Ekiéné arrived with our bags and insisted that we leave immediately, so we climbed in, started up and drove over to the project office. Ekiéné, calling from the window, told the staff that we had to go at once. He thanked them, said he would write and send them a copy of his report and with this we left.

It took nearly three-quarters of an hour to get back to the main north-south trunk road. As I turned off the rutted side road onto the broad carriageway, I saw a figure standing beside the road watching us. It was the same weird man we thought we had left behind at the forestry project.

So unexpected was his appearance that I slowed to look more closely. As I did, he raised his hand and pointed a bony finger at me, mouthing some words that remained unheard in the noise of the Land Rover's engine. I now shared Ekiéné's worry and however much I hoped there might be some logical explanation, I feared there would be none. This man clearly was a sorcerer, but why was he interested in us, and was it me or Ekiéné who was the focus of his attention?

We had one more development project to visit on our way back to Lomé, but neither Ekiéné nor I felt inclined to do so. When we reached the turning, Ekiéné, who was driving at the time, drove straight past. I raised no objection for I too was now keen to get back to the city.

WHEN WE REACHED Lomé it was late afternoon and Ekiéné asked if I would mind dropping him off at his office. We would meet again at the beginning of the following week. I dropped him and drove across the city to my house by the Ghana border.

Lucien's creeper had grown incredibly fast in my absence. Clément had done his best to keep it under control, but had been reluctant to cut anything off, so it had gone rampant with numerous tendrils waving in the sultry sea breeze. As I drove in through the gate the creeper appeared to shimmer. As soon as I had disembarked, I went and looked at it more closely. The whole plant was covered with thousands upon thousands of tiny green butterflies; it was their wings fluttering that caused the shimmering that had attracted my attention. It was remarkably beautiful, but when I realised there were no butterflies on any other plant in the garden, it seemed slightly unreal. I felt an echo of the unease I had felt under the gaze of the strange man who had dogged our progress south.

Clément came out to see who had arrived and, as he unloaded my bag from the back of the Land Rover, I asked what he thought of the butterflies. Without looking at the creeper he immediately hustled me inside, saying they were bad, very bad and I must not go near or touch them.

"Very bad *gri-gri*," he explained. "I will bring help, but you must stay inside," and without any further explanation, he hurried out.

I looked out of the window, wondering if this and the strange man Ekiéné and I had kept seeing were in any way connected. It was a slightly spooky thought.

When Clément returned, an hour later, he took some spare bed sheets outside and used them to cover the Land Rover, concealing it from view. He told me he had found a witch-doctor who would come to the house the next day and cast spells to protect me. The green butterflies were an indication that someone had employed a sorcerer to attack me.

"Why should anyone want to do this?" I asked.

Clément shrugged. The man he had engaged had told him that this was undoubtedly the case and that he could defend me against the attack. Meanwhile he would have to spend some of my housekeeping money on three bottles of gin, a packet of green candles and some flour. Tomorrow he would also need 5,000 CFA (£7.93) to pay the witch-doctor.

Clément would say no more about either the man he had engaged or the threat that he believed had been made against me. He cooked me an excellent supper and asked how the rest of my trip had been and I, in turn, asked about his family and what had been going on in Lomé in my absence. I didn't really listen to his replies as part of my mind was still churning over the strange events of the last few days. I went to bed that night feeling slightly apprehensive, not quite reassured by Clément's calm, matter-of-fact approach to an unusual problem. It wasn't the first time I had come across sorcery of this sort and I knew better than to imagine I was immune to it, but I could think of no reason why anyone here should want to attack me.

After breakfast the next morning I was looking out of the window and saw a thin brown snake winding its way across the bare patch of ground I called my lawn. Curiosity immediately took me outside to look at it. As I bent over to pick it up I heard a shout form the house and Clément came rushing out waving a machete, pushed me aside and with one swipe chopped off the snake's head.

"Why did you do that?" I asked, slightly taken aback, because he knew I was accustomed to picking up snakes and other animals.

"Because it is *gri-gri*," he said, picking up the remains of the snake and showing it to me.

To my utter astonishment it was nothing more than a slightly bendy brown stick, and yet I had seen it travel at least twenty feet across the garden – the marks left in the dust by its passage were

The lizard fetish left on the author's doorstep.

still there! But there was no denying that Clément was only holding a stick and there had been no sleight of hand. I went back into the house muttering about it being high time his mate the witch-doctor turned up to remove whatever curse had been put on me.

Intending to do some work on planning a trip to Mali, I decided to get some maps from the Land Rover and opened the front door. Before I could go through it, Clément called urgently from behind me.

"Don't go out there!"

I turned to ask why and he grabbed my arm and pulled me back inside, pointing with his free hand at the doorstep. There lay a big fat gecko with its arms, legs, tail and eyes missing; it was covered in ants. While there was nothing particularly odd about a dead lizard being covered in scavenging ants, this one somehow looked wrong. Firstly it gave the impression of being laid out like a ritual sacrifice, right in the middle of the doorstep where I should certainly have put my foot. Secondly, it was not dead and its injuries bore all the hallmarks of having been deliberately inflicted. Apart from being sinister, it was slightly revolting.

"You are being attacked from all sides," Clément told me. "You will have to stay in the house until the sorcerer comes to lift the curse."

"When will that be?" I asked.

"He said today, at three o'clock."

"I wasn't going out, I just need some maps from the Land Rover," I said.

"Then I will get them," Clément offered. He went to the door and stepped over the lizard, being careful to avoid touching that step and went over to the Land Rover. As he lifted the cover to open the door he gave a sharp bark of alarm. "Ayie! Someone is very cross with you. They have attacked even your car."

He took a duster that was hanging from his back pocket and used it to cover the handle as he opened the driver's door. From where I stood, just inside the front door, I could see that the whole front seat was covered in a pale yellow powder.

"You cannot have the maps," Clément told me, "They too are covered in this powder," Clément said. "Before you can use them they must be purified."

I wished his tame sorcerer would hurry up and arrive.

The morning passed agonisingly slowly. Clément insisted that I should remain in the house while he went out to buy the gin, the flour and green candles that the sorcerer had said would be needed. When he came back he busied himself in the kitchen preparing lunch, so I saw little of him for a few hours. I sat in my office and tried to work, but concentration was elusive and I found myself going ever more frequently to look out of the window.

As the appointed hour approached, I was again gazing towards the gate, as much anxious as curious to see who would come and what he would do. At precisely three o'clock, there was a sharp rapping on the front door. It made me jump because, although I had been watching, I hadn't seen anyone come through the gate or approach the house.

Clément was ahead of me and I got another shock when he opened the door. The man standing on my front doorstep was the same strange man that had dogged our journey all the way from Bafilo in the far north, hundreds of kilometres down to the forestry project at Eniyé.

"Shut the door!" I called, "That's the sorcerer I told you had been following me and Ekiéné."

"I know," Clément replied. "That is what I employed him to

do, three days ago." He stepped back and invited the man into the house. "Those green butterflies appeared on the creeper outside the day after you went away. I did not know what they were, but Analou told me they were magic that was sent to attack you because someone has laid a curse on you," he continued, explaining. "I was worried, so I went to find someone to help you. This man is a big sorcerer who has been guarding you. He has come now to find this curse and stop it."

"But how could he be in Lama Kara and three other places so fast? He did not have a car, and doesn't look to me like the kind of person who can even drive." I protested, trying to make sense of what he was telling me.

"He is a sorcerer," was the only reply I got. Clément turned to the man and they had a rapid conversation in their own language. The man asked several questions and Clément answered them before turning back to me. "You must show him the house and show him everything. While you are doing this you must tell everything you know about the man who went with you to Lama Kara. You must also tell him of any disagreement you have had recently with this man or with someone else."

The sorcerer took hold of my left hand, gesturing for me to lead him round the house. His hand was icy cold, despite the warm day, and a strange shiver passed down my spine. I also felt a compulsion to do as I had been asked, so I led him towards the inner doorway and we made a tour of every room, opening every cupboard and drawer so that the sorcerer could peer inside. All the time he kept hold of my left hand.

Looking back at this now, I can hear my western friends saying I was mad to show him everything like this. He could just have been a con man scouting the place before coming back to rob me, but somehow I knew this was not the case. This man had something about him and it never occurred to me to do anything other than show him what he wanted to look at. It wasn't just naïvete; I knew I should trust him.

When we had finished the inside tour, he opened the back door and led me outside to make a similar tour of the garden. The marks of the stick-snake's passage across the dusty yard were still clear to see, and the bendy stick still lay where Clément had dropped it. A small knobbly bit, which was the head Clément had hacked off, lay nearby. The sorcerer, still holding my hand in his icy grip, paused to scrutinise these before continuing round the side of the house. He stopped outside the front door and examined the gruesome gecko carefully, poking it with the index finger of his free hand. I noticed that his fingernail was untrimmed and had grown into a talon, almost an inch beyond the tip of his finger. The ants had finally killed the unfortunate lizard and it had now lost its lustre. It looked very dead and was slightly less sinister.

When he had finished with the outside of house, the sorcerer made another tour of the garden on his own, examining the boundaries and looking at all the shrubs and other plants. Coming back to the front wall, he paused at the gate and looked closely at the creeper, its long tendrils still coated with thousands of little green butterflies, shimmering in the afternoon sunlight.

He turned and said something unintelligible to Clément, who was watching us from the house. Clément disappeared inside and emerged a few moments later with a full shopping bag and one of the mixing bowls from his kitchen. He handed these to the sorcerer who put the bag on the ground and said something else.

"He says you must keep touching him or something he is holding all the time until he smacks your hand away," Clément explained. "This is important for his magic. First you must give him the five thousand francs."

I pulled the crisp notes from my pocket and handed them to the sorcerer. He took my hand and placed it on his shoulder, saying words I could not understand but whose meaning was very clear. I curled my fingers round his bony shoulder and took a good grip.

Pulling off Clément's covering of sheets and letting them drop to the ground, the sorcerer placed the bowl and the carrier bag on the bonnet of the Land Rover and began his ritual to counter the gri-gri that had been laid against me. With a throw away lighter, he lit one of the candles, melted its base and stood it on the bonnet in front of the spare wheel which was mounted there, mumbling unintelligible words as he worked. Next he took three handfuls of flour and threw them with some force into the mixing bowl, again accompanying his actions with staccato incantations. He took one of the bottles of gin and broke its top off by knocking it against the vehicle's bumper before sprinkling a little on the ground and pouring about half the contents into the mixing bowl with the flour. This is going to be an interesting cake, I thought.

The incantations continued for a minute or more as the sorcerer stood, staring at the mixing bowl in a trance-like state. I watched in amazement as its contents began to foam. Then, holding the bowl in one hand, he transferred my hand from his shoulder to the bowl with his free hand, before picking up a second green candle and lighting it. He put this in my other hand and made stirring motions towards the mixture in the bowl.

Holding the candle just below the neck, I started stirring the mixture with its stump as he continued his incantations and lit a third candle which he held beneath the bowl. We both still had hold of the bowl with one hand and I could feel his grip as the bowl tilted this way and that in opposition to my stirring. Slowly the mixture stopped foaming and turned into a thin paste as the gin mixed in and the pitch of the sorcerer's incantation rose correspondingly.

It was all very subtle and I had to admit he was a consummate performer. There was no doubting this man for he had about him an aura of power. When Ekiéné and I had seen him before, he had only seemed odd and unusual. He had given the impression of something slightly menacing, but with neither direct nor implied threat to us personally. Now that feeling was gone and what emanated from him was authority, strong and positive. Coupled with the knowledge that he had appeared before at Clément's behest and that he was now employed to cure a curse that had been laid against me, I found his presence strangely reassuring.

When the mixture was stirred to the sorcerer's satisfaction, he stubbed out the candle he was holding beneath the bowl by pushing it against the bottom of the bowl. He took the candle I had been using to stir and inverted this in the mixture, dropping it and his own candle into the paste. More gin was added and I felt the pressure of his hand tipping the bowl. It seemed to rotate so that the stuff in the bottom began to swirl. When the pressure of his grip eased and the bowl was again steady, the mixture continued to swirl, getting faster and faster as I watched it. The contents slowly turned a pale green colour.

It seemed about to spill over the side of the bowl when the sorcerer blew out the green candle that he had placed on the bonnet of the Land Rover with an explosive breath. I was momentarily distracted from the bowl as he snatched the candle and dropped it into the mixture. When I looked at the bowl again its contents were completely still and there was no sign of any of the three candles.

Indicating that I should go with him, the sorcerer walked around the Land Rover and stopped beside the driver's door. He opened it and looked inside. The seat and the floor in the driver's foot well were still covered in the yellow powder I had seen the previous afternoon. Dipping his talon like forefinger into the bowl, the sorcerer flicked some of his mixture onto the seat and the floor. He smeared some around the steering wheel and on the gear levers, hand brake and pedals as well as on the door and window catches, punctuating his continuous chanted spells with a sharp exclamation as he touched each item.

After the Land Rover, he turned his attention to the house. When he scattered some mixture on the front doorstep the dead lizard, still covered in busy black ants, seemed to evaporate. I looked very closely, but the step was undoubtedly clear and he had not been close enough to touch either it or the lizard. We moved round the house and he paused at one of the windows, flicking some of his mixture onto the window sill before moving on. He looked at all the other windows as well, but did nothing to them and I wondered what had singled out that one for his attention. Perhaps someone had tried to gain entry through there?

Next the sorcerer turned his attention to the stick that still lay in the back garden. He dripped mixture onto it from his talon and smeared some on the knobbly lump that Clément had hacked off with his machete. He treated the back door, smearing paste on the step and the doorposts as well as the door itself. This done, he completed the circuit and we went back to the Land Rover.

There was only a little of the mixture left by this time and he added more gin, stirring it in with his clawed finger. When he was satisfied with the consistency, which was much thinner now, he led me towards the garden wall, swathed in rampant creeper and shimmering green butterflies. As we walked along it, both still holding the bowl, his clawed finger dipped and flicked towards the creeper again and again. When we had gone along the inside on both sides of the gate, he led me out into the road and treated the whole outside in the same way, before leading me back to the gate.

He poured the final bit of the thin mixture in a narrow line directly across the open gateway then transferred my hand that had been holding the bowl back to his shoulder as he led me back to stand once more in front of the Land Rover, where he placed the bowl on the bonnet. There was only a very small patch of white residue in the bottom of the bowl which was otherwise quite clean. The sorcerer tipped the last cupful of the gin from the bottle into the bowl, swirled it round with his finger and indicated that I should swallow it.

Pink gin I enjoy, but I wasn't so sure about this. Where had the three green candles gone? Were they somehow dissolved in this? What would this do to my guts? I picked up the bowl, tilted it and swallowed the lot in one go. It was truly disgusting and tasted like alcoholic liquid soap. The sorcerer nodded approvingly, smacked my hand from his shoulder and then placed it on my chest, nodding again. I took this to mean that I no longer had to hold onto him.

There remained just the merest drop of gin in the bottle, which this extraordinary man now tipped into the bowl. He sloshed it round and upended it to splash onto the Land Rover's bonnet and bumper. Taking another bottle of gin from the shopping bag, he carefully unscrewed the top and tipped half of the spirit into the bowl. From a pocket he produced a small leather pouch and sprinkled a quantity of powder on top of the gin, which fizzed slightly and immediately turned a bright rusty red.

The sorcerer's chanting incantation had ended when he upended the last of the first mixture over the Land Rover. For the last few moments he had worked in silence, but now he began a new chant. This had a different timbre which felt very warm and comforting while being slightly menacing. It sounds daft now, sitting in front of a keyboard, to describe it like this but I can still remember the feeling most vividly and this was how I recorded it in my notebook later that evening.

I should not have been surprised when the sorcerer picked up the bowl, offered it to me and indicated, by making slurping noises and hand gestures, that I should take three good sips. When I had done so, he gestured that I should stay where I was, took the bowl from me and set off to repeat the tour of the house and garden that we had made together, flicking some of this new mixture onto each of same targets as he had marked with the previous concoction. When he got back to me there remained less than a cupful in the bowl. He flicked some over the front of the vehicle and tipped the rest on my feet and the ground where I stood.

With this final decantation his performance paused and I thought he was done, but no, there was still one more act to follow. He removed the other bottle of gin from the shopping bag and opened it. This time he took a long draught himself, consuming almost half the bottle before replacing the stopper and stuffing it inside his clothing. He said something to me and then, seeing that I did not understand, called Clément out to translate. There followed a long stream of what could only be instructions, punctuated with emphatic gestures and pointing.

"He says you must go into the house and not come out for one hour," Clement explained. "During that time you must sit with your feet in a bucket of water, up to your ankles. When one hour is over you must come out from the back door and walk twice round the house and twice round your Land Rover. You must spit on the front doorstep before returning inside the house by the back door." He paused and looked at the sorcerer, who spoke again, then bent down and, with his finger, scratched what must have been magic symbols in the dirt across the inside of the gateway. This gruesome claw seemed to have a multiplicity of uses, I thought as I watched.

"You must only enter or leave the house by the back door for three days." Clément continued. "If any visitors come here they must enter and leave the same way. On the fourth day you must take the striped stick that you keep in the Land Rover and beat the creeper on the front wall, all along on both sides. After that, the curse will be finished and you will be protected against other curses." He looked again at the sorcerer, expecting more, but the man had finally finished.

"*Fini*," the man said, confirming this and made as if to leave.

I thanked him for his work and for his protection and offered him my hand, not sure if one was supposed to shake hands with such a man as this. He ignored the gesture, tapped me three times on the chest with his strange multi-functional claw and headed for the gate where he turned and said something else that was as unintelligible as most of his words.

"What did he say?" I asked Clément, turning to speak to him as he was standing slightly behind me.

"I don't know. They were magic words," he replied.

When I turned back to the man, the gateway was empty. The sorcerer had vanished. I went into the house, by the back door, and followed his instructions. I had quite a lot of paper work to catch up on and spent the next three days, quietly at home, doing this while Clément kept me well fed. It was useful time and I managed to complete almost all my outstanding admin tasks. My only visitor was Antoine, who came in from next door to tell me that he and his Zambian girlfriend, whom I had yet to meet, were going to get married and he wanted to invite me to the event. He promised to bring her round in a few days, when she came back from Lusaka, where she had gone to visit her family.

Antoine had, of course, come in by the back door and had noticed the strange marks on the door posts. I told him all about the curse and the sorcerer's visit. When I described the man, he knew immediately who I was talking about. The man was well known to be a powerful sorcerer. I was lucky to have his protection.

This response surprised me as Antoine was a good Catholic and I had no idea that he might also be as receptive to such traditional beliefs. At the same time, I knew from my own experience over years in Africa that there are many inexplicable phenomena and that its sorcerers and witch-doctors can do strange and wonderful things, so why not?

On the fourth day, I went out to get my striped stick from the Land Rover. As I opened the door, I noticed that the inside had been cleaned and thought that it was kind of Clément to have done this for me. I took the stick and did as the sorcerer had bid me, whacking the creeper all along the front wall, inside and out on both sides of the front gate. The creeper was shimmering with its mantle of little green butterflies, but the moment my stick struck the foliage the shimmering stopped as if a switch had been thrown. I looked more closely and there was not a butterfly to be seen, yet nothing had fallen from the creeper and nothing had flown away. The butterflies just weren't there any more.

Remembering the sorcerer's instructions and the very definite way in which he had delivered them, I continued hitting the creeper until I had done what he said. Then I went back to the house to thank Clément for cleaning the Land Rover.

"I have not touched it," he said. "It is clean because the sorcerer removed the curse."

I wondered what the sorcerer had said to Clément as he was leaving – words that Clément had denied understanding – and decided it might be better not to know.

5 ~ A lakeside liaison

THE REQUEST CAME FROM the presidential palace in Lomé. It required me to present myself at the Hotel du Lac at Anécho, on the shore of Lac Togo, for a meeting with Monsieur Kountumene and Monsieur Atunyola, two of the President's special representatives. The purpose of the meeting was to explore the problem of providing regular clean drinking water supplies for the fishing communities around the lake. The public health officials in the area were concerned at the frequency of minor outbreaks of waterborne diseases and had been instructed to address the issue. Since funding was provisionally available, the President had decided to act.

I was known to the government through my involvement in water-related projects in northern Togo and had once been introduced to President Etienne Eyadema by another President while attending a third President's banquet in Senegal. Given all this, and the fact that I was currently based in Lomé, it was hardly a surprise to have been asked to assist with setting up the project.

Monsieur Kountumene and Monsieur Atunyola were already there when I arrived at the Hotel du Lac half an hour before the

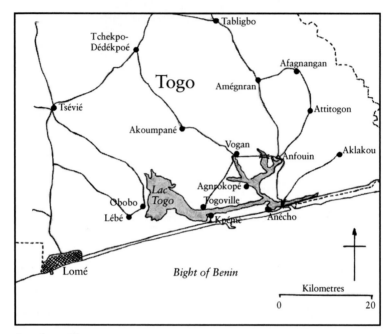

Southern Togo.

appointed time. They were smart young men, a little older than me, dressed in elegant safari suits. One wore blue and the other brick red, both with immaculately polished shoes. They took me to a comfortable seating area overlooking the lake and called for coffee. Producing a series of maps, they showed me the location and size of the various communities around the lakeside and proceeded to explain the details of the problem that they had been charged to resolve.

These two men were very efficient and I was impressed by their briefing even if their style was a bit stiff and formal, as indeed were their personalities. When they had said what they wanted to and I had asked a few questions, they proposed that we visit some of the communities to see the problems at first hand. They already had a boat standing by, complete with a boatman to drive it.

I agreed and they excused themselves, saying that they needed to change into more appropriate attire for going boating. I looked at my own clothes and decided to go out to my Land Rover and change my shoes. The rest of me would do. As for the two Togolese, they returned wearing knee-length shorts, soft rubber sandals and brightly patterned printed cotton shirts with heavily machined embroidery around the neck and short sleeves. Both men had big straw hats and mirror sunglasses. They looked like a caricature pair of Miami dudes on furlough.

Tied up at the hotel jetty was a battered fibreglass speedboat powered by a pair of huge outboard engines. The boatman lounged nearby. He was a sour looking man in a faded blue corduroy flat cap, with only two front teeth and a half-smoked cigarette hanging from his lip. He looked like a well-toasted, slightly moth-eaten version of Andy Capp. All he lacked was the bottle of stout sticking out of his back pocket.

As we climbed aboard, he asked a question in his own language, Ewe, and gave me a long speculative look when he received an answer from Monsieur Kountumene who was clearly in charge of this little outing. His whole demeanour changed as soon as he started the outboards; any resemblance to a cartoon character went out the window as he metamorphosed smoothly into a highly skilled and professional boatman.

He swiftly released and coiled the ropes that tied us to the jetty; overboard went the fag-end. He checked that we were all safely seated before easing the throttles forward. A smart sailing cap appeared from somewhere. When he jammed it on his head, he looked the part of the skipper. He even smiled as we moved slowly away from the jetty. When he opened the throttles fully, the boat rose cleanly out of the water and leapt forward.

I thought the trip would be short if we were going to travel at this speed; the far shore was not far away and we were approaching it at alarming speed. The lake appeared to be small enough for us to see almost all of it from our starting point. This, of course, was a false impression. It might have been sensible for me to have checked the map beforehand. As we drew nearer to the far shore, a small creek became visible and the boatman headed straight for this. We powered up the creek for a couple of kilometres, our wake sloshing a wave of half a metre along the shore on either side.

We continued like this until the creek opened up a bit. A branch went off to the left. Ignoring this, we drove onwards for fully five minutes before the shores began to recede still further and the channel became a broad highway with bobbing floats and the frames of fish traps along either side. Soon we saw *pirogues* hauled up on the left hand bank. The boat slowed and we cruised gently in towards the shore, stopping when the bow grounded softly on a sandy beach to one side of a very narrow and rickety looking jetty.

"Agnrokopé," announced our boatman, pointing to a collection of reed huts fifty metres from the water, where nets were hung to dry on poles that had been pushed into the sand. "There are eleven fishing families here," he continued in excellent French, "and the main village is situated half a kilometre from the lake, behind those trees." He pointed to a line of tall Doum palms standing high above some thick bushes.

The boatman made fast and the rest of us climbed out and stepped cautiously along the flimsy jetty to the sand. Three fishermen emerged from one of the reed huts and stood staring at us. Monsieur Atunyola called a greeting and headed in their direction. After several minutes of discussion, he turned round and beckoned us over. "The fishermen have agreed to take us to their village and introduce us to the headman," he explained.

The village was a mixture of huts made in the traditional style, with mud walls and conical thatched roofs. A few were built of grey concrete blocks with shiny silver roofs of galvanised wriggly tin. These looked new. We were told they were owned by villagers who worked in the city and had built them for their families with the money they brought back.

The village headman was a nondescript fellow, clearly a fisherman himself. His hands, showing long experience of being immersed in water, bore the scars that handling and mending nets over many years tends to inflict. He was friendly enough and very willing to tell us about their water problems once Monsieur Kountumene had explained the reason for our visit. In fact it was difficult to get him to stop talking and let us ask a few questions.

We were there for forty minutes, during which time the headman, with a trail of curious villagers following, gave us a detailed tour of his village and showed us where they drew their water and where they dumped their waste. Monsieur Kountumene had come equipped with all the necessary kit, so we took samples and made our escape, promising to be back and to help them clean up their water supply.

As the boatman steered us away from Agnrokopé, Monsieur Atunyola had a long discussion with him in Ewe. The purpose of this, he told me once it was concluded, was to get him to take us to a few representative communities, while just pointing out all the others, and not to land us with too many like the headman we had just encountered. The boatman knew all the fishermen well, having spent the whole of his life on the lake, and should make a useful guide now that he understood what was needed. After Monsieur Atunyola's explanation, he seemed discernibly more enthusiastic.

I had discovered the boatman spoke good French; now I discovered that his name was Nougré. We chatted as we travelled on up the lake.

"What do you normally do with your boat?" I asked.

He explained that it belonged to the Hotel du Lac and he was employed to take tourists out on the lake, either just for a ride, or so that they could go fishing. "It is very boring work. Most of the time the boat is tied up, waiting for customers." If it wasn't for the salary, which was small but regular, he would have abandoned the job long ago.

He had once been a lake fisherman himself, he told me. The living was a bit precarious, particularly if you had a family. Nougré had eleven children, so he needed a regular income to feed them all and to send them to school. He brightened up even more when I told him that if I was engaged to carry out the project that we were currently exploring, I would insist on having him as my boatman and would make sure that the government paid him a proper salary for the work.

Shortly after we left Agnrokopé, the lake widened still further to become a much more sizeable body of water, but still not large. When I mentioned this to Nougré, he laughed. "This is only the small bit of Lac Togo. We will go back to the other part after we have seen the villages up between Afidégniban and Anfouin."

I tried to repeat these two names and got my tongue tangled, to the amusement of the other three men. However much I tried, Ewe was always a difficult language and probably the one of which I learned the least in all my travels. It sounded easy when the locals spoke it, and I eventually understood quite a lot, but I never managed to say much that anyone could understand.

We inspected six more fishing communities, mostly from the lake, before Nougré turned the boat around and opened the throttles wide. It took an exciting twenty minutes to get back to the fork that we had bypassed earlier and here he turned west. Nougré told us about the lake as we raced along and I realised that it was actually much larger than it appeared, extending nearly twenty kilometres from end to end. The part we were now entering opened wide a few kilometres further in and was over twenty metres deep in the middle.

Nougré stopped the boat at Kpémé and took us ashore to find lunch. This was more than a village, being only a kilometre off the main coastal highway. There was a small restaurant on the shore. Our boatman obviously knew the proprietor well and I guessed he must regularly bring his clients here to eat. It was easy to see why: the food, to suit both indigenous and French tastes, was excellent.

After lunch we visited three more fishing villages up near the top of the lake where Nougré knew they had problems with their water supplies. He pointed out many more small settlements around the shore as we passed, and told us a bit about each.

It was getting towards sunset as we headed back towards Anécho, still at full power, even though the boat had no lights. Nougré was confident that he knew where he was and that we would not hit anything.

"None of the fishermen will be out on the water after dark in case some evil spirit comes out of the lake and snatches them," he explained when I asked him if he always travelled so fast at night. "At night the lake belongs to me." I believed him.

Back at the hotel, Monsieur Kountumene paid for the hire of

the boat and I slid Nougré an extra thousand franc note – about £1.60. As we headed for the hotel, he pulled out a sponge and began washing down the boat.

We sat down with a beer in the hotel bar overlooking the lake to discuss the information we had gathered. After half an hour, it was clear that we could make a major impact on the problem by simply providing good filters in most of the communities. There would need to be some health education, but a public health campaign was due to start soon in this area.

I sketched out some ideas and drew simple diagrams illustrating how sub-sand extraction filters worked, to help the two men understand what I had in mind. They seemed surprised that the solution could be so cheap and simple. Calling for more beer, Monsieur Atunyola excused himself for a moment, saying he had to ring his boss and let him know how we had got on. I thought no more about this and carried on explaining something to Monsieur Kountumene.

When Monsieur Atunyola returned from making his phone call, it was to tell us that his boss was very pleased with the report and wanted to hear about it first hand from me as soon as possible. "He will meet us at the restaurant in Kpémé in one hour's time," said Monsieur Kountumene. "You can explain your plan to him over supper."

Nougré had already been warned and was standing by outside to take us all back to Kpémé.

I spent a brief moment hoping that I was not going to have to pay for the meal, as I didn't have a lot of cash with me, and then resigned myself. These were government people and we were on government business. The invitation had come from a government official, so he could deal with the bill. We climbed into the boat again and a very happy boatman treated us to another of his white-knuckle specials in the dark.

It didn't take long for us to get to Kpémé again. Nougré cut the power and took us gently in towards the landing stage. The place looked different in the dark and I was surprised to find an armed policeman waiting for us on the jetty. He pointed a bright torch at us until Monsieur Atunyola announced himself and told the man to point it elsewhere. Even so, he gave me a close inspection before he let me step ashore. This didn't bother me, but I was surprised to see a lot of other policemen outside the restaurant and several more standing about just inside the door.

I was going to ask why there were so many policemen here when Monsieur Kountumene steered me into the dining room and introduced me to his boss, who was none other than the President of Togo, Etienne Eyadema. If I hadn't previously met him, this would really have astounded me, but at that first short meeting he had asked for a copy of my report on the Senegal River project that dealt with very similar problems and this, presumably, was his response. It did seem rather unorthodox, all the same, as this man was widely reputed to be one who made a cult out of ceremony and respect for his status and position. Presidents, particularly this one, do not habitually meet unimportant rural development agents at out-of-the-way restaurants after dark, so this was surprising. I realised that I should have asked my two companions who their boss was. Ah well, perhaps I was less easily thrown by unexpected events now and I was getting used to the interesting surprises that West Africa served up.

After a brief greeting, the President invited me to a table where a large-scale map of Lac Togo was spread out. He wanted to know everywhere we had been and who we had seen in each place. He enquired in detail about the water problems in the villages where we had gone ashore and was quick to pick up on any differences. I brought out my notebook so that I could read off the facts, aware that later he would certainly double check everything I told him with his two agents.

I was impressed by the level of his interest and by how well-informed he already was about the lakeside communities. It shouldn't really have surprised me because he was, after all, the leader of a very small nation and, if my two companions today were anything to go by, he had an army of smart people gathering information and keeping him informed. He asked some searching questions about my projects in other parts of the country, particularly the one up near Lama Kara. Later, I learned that was his home region and part of the project was even based in Pyo, where he had been born.

The detail with which he controlled the country became clear when his questions revealed that he was even aware of my having brought an American called Arnie Slomann from Niger to help the forest people of Amézodjikopé with their springs. Apart from the formalities of getting Arnie's visa sorted out, the government had no contact with this project, it having been a private initiative on the part of the village headman who asked me for help.

The President asked me how I thought this project should proceed, how it would fit in with his public health programme and what I thought it would cost. At this point I decided it would be wise to change the subject. I needed time to sit down with my notebook and a map like the one before us on the table, to consider the possibilities. "It will take time to work it all out properly," I said, "but I should be able to submit a detailed report and recommendations to your office within a week."

"Good, then let's have some food," he said, and led me towards the dining area where a table had been laid for dinner. His two young agents were included in the invitation, as was a man who had been listening carefully throughout our discussion but who had not yet been introduced. He told me his name was Gnasingyé Goukanigyu and that he was the director designate of the public health programme that was just waiting for the President's final approval before being launched. This man clearly had a lot of technical questions of his own that he wanted to ask, but the President had other fish to fry.

He wanted to talk about football, for the Togolese team were doing well in a pan-African competition and he was proud of them and wanted to hear other people sing their praises. I know nothing about football and take absolutely no interest in it, but the local papers and radio had been full of news about this competition for the previus week. It had been hard to ignore and somehow I must have picked up one or two of the names of the team's heroes. I tossed these into the conversation, saying they must be good and mentioning the lavish praise the press had heaped on them. The President was a happy man.

The meal was excellent: grilled lake fish and *foufou*, laced with red hot sauce that was like an instant tonsillectomy. My notebook records that we drank a fine Bordeaux wine, and also that the hot pepper sauce utterly destroyed its taste. We finished with a crème brulée that was nowhere near as good as my cook, Clément, produced at home in Lomé. The mixture of ethnic and French cuisine might have appeared incongruous, but this was hardly a normal dinner party. There were no other diners in the place, the restaurant was surrounded by policemen and half the party had arrived by speedboat.

After the meal, the President declined coffee, explaining that he had ministers waiting for him in Lomé. "I shall look forward to reading your report next week," he said as he shook my hand. Then his policemen coalesced around him and he was swept outside to a waiting limousine and driven away.

Still feeling slightly amazed by the whole experience, I turned round to find Monsieur Goukanigyu, eager to arrange another meeting. He had many things to discuss and would like to meet me without any of the President's men there. I invited him to come and see me at my house in the morning and to bring along a copy of the programme he was going to run. I felt an instant liking for this man and was certain that he could be very helpful.

Since the other two were in a huddle of their own, I took the opportunity to ask my new friend a question that had puzzled me all evening. "That was an interesting meeting," I said, "and a complete surprise. I did not expect the President to take such a personal interest, or to meet him like this. Does this happen often?"

"No. He is usually so tied up with state affairs and officials that he cannot escape. Anyway, power changes a man and he is not as approachable as he was. This is a rare event and possible only because everyone here is related to the President, so their loyalty is total."

"What, even you?"

"Even me. He is my brother-in-law," he said, nodding. "Some of the palace women who have pleased him come from Lac Togo, so he wishes to do something for their families. That is why these projects will proceed. But he will probably ask your government to help pay for your work and maybe for mine as well!" He finished with a conspiratorial grin.

Looking across Lac Togo toward Anécho. The lake today is a fraction of its former size due to changing land use and increased demands for fresh water.

Before we left, I managed to take possession of the map that we had studied earlier, rolling it up as we went through the restaurant and out to our boat. Against the odds, Nougré delivered us safely to the Hotel du Lac. He beamed when I told Monsieur Kountumene that in my country it was customary to pay double time for a man who had to work such long hours without notice, especially after dark. I suggested that five thousand francs of the government's money (about £7.93) would be an appropriate sum. Judging by Nougré's reaction, that is what he received. He shook my hand vigorously when we said goodnight.

"Come any time and I will drive for you," he said. "This is the first time I have taken a guest to have dinner with the President. Now I have a very good story to tell my grandsons."

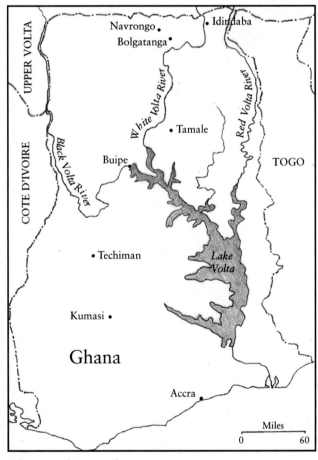

Ghana and its northern game reserve areas.

6 ~ Godfrey's elephants

GODFREY AKEMPULA WAS a man of diverse talents with a passion for big wildlife, particularly elephants. That, and the fact that a long time ago the manager of a game reserve had offered him a job, was why he became a game ranger.

All that had happened in 1959, when Ghana was newly independent and most of the old colonial managers were handing over their responsibilities to Ghanaians. Godfrey was on his way home on holiday from a college at Kintampo in western Ghana, where he was doing a course in forestry. Coming north on a bus as far as Bolgatanga, he then took a ride in a bush taxi to Nangodi, with his bicycle and his small suitcase strapped to the roof rack, along with everyone else's baggage. At Nangodi he tied his suitcase to the pannier rack of his bicycle and set off to pedal the remaining eleven miles to his village. His route took him through the edge of the game reserve.

Godfrey had always been interested in the wild animals living in the bush surrounding his village. Most of the boys in his community knew the names of the more common varieties since, before the reserve was established, their fathers often used to organise hunts for meat. The boys played an active part in the hunt as beaters and by helping to carry home the catch. As a little boy, Godfrey too had done his bit, but as he got older he began to dislike killing things and preferred to watch the animals and birds and to learn something of their ways. As a result, he had often been able to get quite close to animals that the other boys would have scared away by their predatory excitement.

On this particular day, Godfrey noticed a mob of vultures and kites circling some distance ahead above the track he was riding along. They were flying low, so he suspected that some animal must be lying in the bush, either already dead or very near to death. The birds were just waiting for that indefinable moment, which could not be many minutes off, when there was no longer any movement from the animal and death claimed another victim. Then they would swoop down to tear its carcass to bits with their razor-sharp beaks.

As he approached, Godfrey could see a large grey lump lying next to the path. He rang his bell, waved his arms and shouted at the birds as he stopped and laid his bicycle on the ground. Wings flapped, there were angry squawks from the vultures, shrill screams from the kites and the circling mob rose a few dozen feet higher in the hot afternoon air. He looked around at the bush, in case a hyena or jackal had picked up the scent, knowing that if the vultures were landing, other scavengers wouldn't be far behind.

He could see now that the fallen animal was an elephant. He looked around again to see if the rest of the herd were nearby. He knew that these huge beasts had great loyalty to their friends and family, often staying near one that was injured to try and help. He didn't want to be charged by a protective tusker, especially as he meant no harm.

Walking quickly round the stricken beast, he could see that it was quite young; it was female and had a huge open wound in its side, as if it had been gored by a giant bull. It was clear that the elephant also had a broken back leg. Godfrey decided that although there was nothing he could do for the animal himself, he could report it to the game park authorities. The young elephant was still very much alive and, if the vultures would keep away, perhaps she might survive. He tore a few branches off a nearby tree and laid them in a tangle over the open wound, in the hope that they would delay the scavengers and make it more difficult for them to attack the wound.

Then Godfrey picked up his bicycle and set off towards the nearest ranger station. After half a mile he stopped, untied his suitcase and stashed it in the branches of a small thorn tree. He was able to travel much faster without the extra load on the bike and in less than half an hour, he arrived at the ranger station, tired, dusty and with aching legs.

As luck would have it, Robert Kernan, the park manager, was at the station when he arrived, together with two other expatriate rangers, one of whom was a vet. Godfrey had pedalled hard over rough ground and was out of breath, but he managed to convey the urgency of the situation. Mr Kernan loaded the vet and five Ghanaian rangers into the back of a truck, with Godfrey in the cab beside him to tell him where to go. He set off at breakneck speed, back towards where Godfrey had seen the fallen elephant.

The carrion eaters still circled the spot where the animal lay and, as the truck scrunched to a halt in a cloud of red dust, a number took flight with squawks of alarm. Godfrey was distressed to see that a few of the boldest had already landed and sat on what remained of his bundle of sticks, trying to tear fresh flesh from the elephant's wounded side. Their victim was weaker now, barely able to raise her trunk in a feeble effort to ward off the attackers. Her survival was still far from certain, but the end would surely not have been long in coming had the rangers not arrived when they did.

The vet had brought his medical bag and proceeded to inject a number of drugs, including a sedative, into the fallen elephant. Once this was done he cleaned the wound with disinfectant and inspected the damage. Although the wound was large and messy, it had only ripped through the skin and some of the superficial muscles of the abdominal wall. If the guts within had been exposed, it would have meant certain death for the elephant, as infection would rapidly have taken hold. Fortunately, the inner membranes were intact, so the vet dusted the wound with sulphur powder and pulled the sides of it together, inserting a number of tough wire stitches to hold it closed.

As soon as this was done, the other rangers began working a heavy canvas sheet under the beast. By raising her legs, trunk and head with their hands, they could slide the sheet some of the way under. Then by pegging the edge to the ground and pulling on her three uninjured legs, while holding her head up and pushing, they managed, after a few minutes of heaving, to slide the young elephant onto the canvas sheet.

The floor of the truck was made of two layers of heavy planks, specially for loading unwieldy cargoes. The top layer slid out to form a shallow ramp up which the load could be slid. All the rangers had practised this technique but, Godfrey learned later, this was the first time they had tried to do it with a live animal.

Mr Kernan reversed the truck into the right position and the ramp planks were slid out. With a bar pushed through loops along the front edge of the heavy canvas, a cable from a small manual winch, mounted just behind the cab, was attached. Ropes from the far end of the canvas sheet were brought up, over the animal, and tied to the bar. Then with men pushing and pulling, and Mr Kernan cranking the winch handle, the elephant was dragged slowly and steadily up the ramp into the truck.

Once the elephant was safely on board, the ramp planks were dropped into brackets across the rear, to stop anything sliding out, the rangers all climbed aboard and the truck set off back to the ranger station, travelling much slower this time so as not to damage the patient or cause her undue alarm.

Robert Kernan took the opportunity to find out a bit about Godfrey and asked him a lot of questions, both about himself and about the course he was doing at the technical college. As they approached the ranger station, he asked his last question:

"Why did you come to report this elephant?"

"It sick, sah," Godfrey replied. "I want save dis one. Deyah no be ada elefants nearby to help. Deyah only me and I can no do anyting. I hope it maybe you can do somting. Elefants should no go die so young."

"Mmmm," Mr Kernan said, considering this, as he pulled the truck to a halt in front of a strongly stockaded enclosure. "We'll have to try to save it then, won't we."

The injured elephant was unloaded and installed in her new pen. The vet cleaned the wound again, covering it with gooey cream and a dressing, before giving the animal another injection. One of the rangers placed a tin bath of clean water by her trunk and everyone stood back to watch. Godfrey noticed that a splint had been applied to the broken leg which was now bound up with strong bandages.

Gradually the elephant began to move and, after about fifteen minutes, had succeeded in heaving her body upright, although she still lay on the ground. Her trunk, which had been waving about randomly, now sought the water and in a couple of minutes she had drunk all that was in the bath. Her trunk began looking for more, finding none. Without asking, Godfrey picked up the end of the hose that had been used to fill the bath, turned on the tap and walked slowly and directly towards the elephant.

He talked to her quietly as he approached, unaware of the consternation his action had stirred up among the watching rangers. Godfrey put the end of the hose in the bath and let it fill to overflowing. As the young elephant's trunk reached out for another drink, he put his thumb over the end of the pipe and directed a cooling shower of water over the animal. Unperturbed, the animal closed its eyes and carried on sucking up the water from the bath. When she had drunk enough, she directed her trunk toward Godfrey. Some of the rangers gasped in alarm.

Godfrey stood still and continued directing the cooling shower over the elephant's body, taking care not to wash off the cream the vet had applied to the wound. He held out his other hand for the elephant to smell and did not flinch when the end of the trunk curled around his fingers as though to shake hands. As the elephant let go of Godfrey's hand, the rangers relaxed and murmured to one another. They had never seen anything like this.

Godfrey refilled the tin bath and then turned off the hose. He picked up an armful of hay from a pile that the rangers had put next to the stockade and walked slowly back towards the elephant. The animal watched him approach, lifted her trunk to sniff his scent and then explored the hay he placed on the ground beside her head. Moments later she had stuffed a wad of hay into her mouth and started chewing. Godfrey walked back to where the rangers were standing.

"Well, it looks like that elephant is determined to survive," Mr Kernan said to Godfrey. "But it's going to need some looking after. Do you want a job, young man?"

"To lookin afta dis elefant, sah?" asked Godfrey, taken somewhat by surprise.

"Well, you can start with that one, but we've got lots more animals in this park and we need good men as rangers," Mr Kernan replied. "So, do you want the job?"

"Oh yes, sah!" Godfrey said with a huge grin. "I like it very much to work in dis park."

SO IT WAS THAT GODFREY became a game ranger. Mr Kernan took him to the stores and found him a uniform, then sent him to the bunkhouse to find a place to sleep with the other unmarried men. The following morning, he drove Godfrey back to where the elephant had fallen and recovered his suitcase from the thorn tree where he had left it. After that, he and Godfrey walked slowly round the spot, looking for signs that might tell what had happened and maybe explain how the young elephant had been injured. As they walked, Mr Kernan explained to Godfrey what he was looking for and told him what the different signs they found meant. It was Godfrey's first lesson in game management.

Later that week, Mr Kernan drove Godfrey to his village, so that he could see his family and tell them about his new job. His father did not seem surprised when Mr Kernan told him how Godfrey had behaved with the wounded elephant. He was very pleased that his son was now a game ranger and did not seem upset that he would never complete the forestry course. Success at that would have forced him to move south to the forest region to find work; now he would live and work more locally and occasionally come home and see his family.

For the first two weeks, Godfrey's time was largely occupied with looking after the injured elephant. Mr Kernan and the other rangers were amazed that he seemed to have no fear of this wild animal. They were equally amazed at the animal's easy acceptance of Godfrey, as though she knew he was trying to help her. Within a couple of days she was able to stand, although walking was obviously difficult with one leg splinted.

Godfrey cleaned and tended the wound in the elephant's side; a two-foot gash that had ripped through its flank. When she had been brought in, the vet had inserted more strong stitches before giving the elephant the antidote to the tranquilliser which had kept it calm while being transported from the bush. After a week he came to take these stitched out. The elephant stood calmly as Godfrey tended her wound, but became agitated when Ted, the vet, approached.

"Don't be silly girl," Godfrey told the animal. "Missa Ted tryin to help you, like me. Look, he is my friend too." So saying, Godfrey took Ted's hand in his own and held it out towards the elephant's anxiously waving trunk. After that it stood still while Ted removed the stitches, only flinching slightly when one or two pulled at the wound as they were extracted. The last one was a bit more stubborn and Ted had to pull harder. It must have hurt a bit because the elephant swung her trunk round and delivered a sharp slap to Ted's backside that made the watching rangers laugh.

Four days after the injured elephant had been brought to the ranger station, one of the Ghanaian rangers had reported seeing a solitary buffalo cow with blood-stained horns. A posse of rangers set out to track the beast and find out more. It did not take long for them to link this beast to all the buffalo hoof prints that Mr Kernan and Godfrey had found near the spot where the injured elephant had fallen, so now they were fairly sure who the culprit was. The question was: why? Elephants and buffalo normally live side by side without being in competition. Something must have caused the buffalo to attack. And why was the young elephant alone in the bush instead of with her herd? This one was only about six years old, and would never normally be abandoned; even the young bulls would still have been with the herd at that age.

One afternoon, two weeks after Godfrey had started his new job, a farmer who lived not far from the ranger station came in to report that his cows had been injured by a wild animal from the park. He wanted a ranger to come and track it.

Ted and one of the Ghanaian rangers went to the man's farm and found familiar hoof prints all over the place. Three of the man's cows had been slightly gored and one goat had been trampled to death. Compensation would undoubtedly be demanded in due course.

They set out on foot to track the offender but had to turn back, with the approach of dusk, before finding it. As they were passing a small thicket, just a few hundred yards from the farmer's house and stock pen, there was a snort and rustle from the bushes and the two rangers found an angry buffalo charging at them from less than twenty yards.

Ted was fair skinned and he was wearing a light khaki uniform so, even in the waning light, he was still easy to see. The other ranger was, of course, black and dressed in jungle green, and was less distinct in the deepening gloom. He also carried the only rifle. Ted heard the rifle bolt being worked as the buffalo thundered towards him. There was a loud bang and time seemed to go into slow motion.

The buffalo's head dropped, as if it were about to hit its target and it was getting ready to hook and toss. The front feet landed a little short of a full stride and the animal's forequarters seemed to drop as its nose was lowered still further, until almost touching the ground. Then time returned to normal speed.

One moment, a ton of angry buffalo was hurtling towards Ted at something over thirty-five miles an hour. The next, its head was down and the huge body was cart-wheeling, end over end, to slam onto the earth on its back. It skidded to a stop within an arm's length of him. The ranger's aim had been excellent; the bullet had ripped into its heart and the buffalo was already dead before its great body came to a standstill.

The farmer and his family came out to see what was happening, bringing lanterns with them. Soon, other people from nearby houses arrived and a small crowd gathered around the two rangers and the dead beast.

Ted brought knives from his Land Rover and cut the head off the buffalo. He skinned out one leg and removed the haunch to provide meat for the ranger station, giving the rest of the carcass and the hide to the assembled farmers to compensate them for the damage the beast had done to their livestock. Ted and the ranger climbed back into their Land Rover and returned to the ranger station. There was fresh meat for supper that evening and a lot of speculation about what might have caused this lone cow to behave so aggressively.

In the morning, Ted sawed open the buffalo's skull to look at the brain. There he found a massive tumour which he concluded had caused this animal's aberrant behaviour and made it attack even large animals like the elephant. The pressure in its head must have been extremely painful; the ranger's bullet had undoubtedly saved it from greater agonies and from inflicting further injury on other animals or even people.

A week after this episode, the elephant, which had appeared to be healing well, went into a decline. After lunch one day, Godfrey found her leaning against the stockade, head held low, looking decidedly wobbly. Ted had gone off to visit one of the other ranger stations in the park, so Godfrey had to do the best he could on his own.

He used the hose again to cool the animal and brought the tin bath to make sure she had enough water to drink. The young elephant ignored the water and just slumped against the stockade wall. As Godfrey ran his hands over her, he realised that she was hot and feverish. He asked the other rangers what he should do, but none had any useful ideas. Unable to think of anything else, Godfrey kept the hose running to cool the animal and sent one of the others to the office to fetch an umbrella. He stood beside the sick elephant until sunset, shading her head with the umbrella and playing the cooling hose over her body. When the evening meal was ready, another ranger brought Godfrey his food, but still he refused to leave his charge.

He remained beside the elephant until next morning when Ted returned. By then, the elephant was very sick indeed, but the cause was not immediately apparent. The wound in her side was healing well and her leg was no longer as painful as it had been. While still ungainly, with the splints in place, she could at least put some weight on the foot now and no longer flinched when Godfrey ran his hands down the leg. This was something else and needed proper diagnosis. Ted produced a large needle and, without even a flicker of protest from the patient, he drew off a large sample of blood from a vein in the back of her ear. He spent the rest of the morning running tests and examining the sample under a microscope.

After six hours of tests, the vet was no nearer to understanding what had made the elephant sick, but it was obviously something very virulent. Perhaps this explained why the rest of the herd had abandoned her. They might even have done so before she was injured by the buffalo. Elephants seem to have a sixth sense about these things and maybe they were aware that this young female had a sickness which threatened the whole herd. That could have made them abandon her.

Unable to identify what was wrong, Ted injected a massive dose of antibiotics. At the same time he pushed a tube down the elephant's throat and pumped in a powerful laxative, thinking to clean out the whole system. He then fixed up a drip and started pouring fluid and essential salts into her bloodstream. Through all this, Godfrey stayed by his elephant, offering soft words of comfort and encouragement, watching and learning.

To everyone's surprise, the elephant was still alive the following morning and Godfrey had named her Mulanye, meaning 'resilient'.

Still unable to identify the cause of the elephant's sickness, the vet sent samples away to a laboratory in Accra for analysis, but the results would not be back for weeks. He hoped it wouldn't be too late, but said nothing of his doubts to Godfrey.

For the next three days, Godfrey stayed beside Mulanye, changing the infusion bags as the vet had shown him, soothing and caressing her, telling her in a low monologue what a fine beast she was and how she would soon get better. Having saved her from the carrion eaters, he was determined not to lose her now to some unidentified sickness. In all that time, he left her side only once, just for a few minutes, to organise some materials with which to build an awning to shade Mulanye from the heat of the sun. Once it was erected, he looked at the sky, hoping not to see the circling shapes of vultures. They always seemed to know when an animal on the ground was mortally afflicted, but the sky remained clear.

"Dem vulcha no tink you go die," he told Mulanye, loudly. "So now you muss get betta; ah'm tellin you!"

By the following morning, the young elephant had shown definite signs of improvement and her trunk sought out the tin bath Godfrey had kept filled with fresh water. Over the next few days the sickness, which was still a mystery, left her and Mulanye began to take more notice of her surroundings, including Godfrey. When he offered bunches of fresh hay, she took them gently with her trunk and stuffed them in her mouth. The other rangers noticed that her trunk then caressed Godfrey's arm or shoulder as if to say 'Thank you' for the morsel. It became obvious that an intense and deep bond had formed between Godfrey and the elephant. As she recovered, whenever he moved from her side, she watched him intently and, if he strayed too far, she followed him.

It was ten days before Godfrey returned to the bunkhouse to sleep. In the middle of the night the rangers were woken by an extraordinary noise. They rushed outside in time to see the stockade of Mulanye's pen come crashing down and the young elephant walk out of the gap waving her trunk and sniffing the night air. The moment she detected Godfrey, she shuffled over and wrapped her trunk around him, rumbling deeply to show her satisfaction at finding him.

Godfrey started talking softly to the elephant, running his hands over her trunk and forelegs to make sure that she had not hurt herself while breaking down the stockade. Then he led her back to the enclosure. When he tried to leave her again, Mulanye made to follow him. It was obvious that she wanted him to stay with her and was not going to be left alone. Godfrey asked the other rangers to bring him a camp bed and settled down to sleep under the awning at the side of Mulanye's pen. The young elephant stood beside him, munching hay, rumbling and occasionally caressing Godfrey with the tip of her trunk.

In the morning, while the other rangers repaired the stockade, Godfrey took Mulanye over to the pen's gate and showed her how to open it. "You muss not breakin him fence," he told Mulanye, with a wagging finger. "Iss deyah to protect you, not to make you prisnah. Ifin you want come out, you open diss gate like ebrywan else."

It is difficult to imagine an elephant looking sheepish, but that is what the other rangers reported when recounting this incident. From then on, Mulanye opened the gate to her own pen and strolled out whenever she felt the need for Godfrey's company. He had to give her a number of similar lectures on her behaviour so that she would stay put and allow him to get on with his other duties, for he was now a national park ranger, not merely an elephant minder and he had other responsibilities.

FOUR MONTHS AFTER Godfrey had found the injured elephant, she was well enough to be released. The wound from the buffalo's horn had healed well, although she would always bear a very visible scar down her right flank. The broken bone had mended, the splints had been removed and, although still needing to regain some strength, her leg was moving normally and taking full weight. Of the sickness that had caused so much alarm, there was no evidence. The samples sent to Accra had revealed nothing of its cause, so more samples had been forwarded to London for further investigation. It was time for Mulanye to go back to the wild.

The herd to which Mulanye was thought to belong was located by the rangers and plans were made. On the day appointed for her release, the rangers brought a large lorry with tall sides and parked it with the open back pushed up against an earthen ramp next to the elephant pen. Mulanye made it very plain that she did not trust the lorry and had no wish to embark but, eventually, with a bit of coaxing from Godfrey and the gift of a few fresh loaves of bread strewn along the ramp, she was coaxed into this new conveyance and the rear gate was closed. The twenty-mile journey to where the herd was located took over two hours. Scouts had been out earlier, assessing the direction in which the herd was moving, as it was planned to drop Mulanye ahead of them. Another ramp was assembled from heavy planks and the back gates of the lorry were opened. Once again, loaves and a tin bath of cool water were used to lure the beast out and away from the lorry.

Once unloaded, Mulanye just stood there, looking confused and uncertain. Godfrey stood beside her, stroking her trunk and talking softly. Eventually he patted her on the cheek and told her to stay there and wait for her herd, then he walked away and climbed into the truck. As the driver moved the lorry away, the elephant turned to watch where it went and seemed about to follow. She looked around at the four or five other rangers, who stood in a ring around her, and flapped her ears.

The men withdrew, all in different directions, moving several hundred yards away into the scrub before circling round to the lorry which was waiting for them, out of sight of the elephant. Half an hour later, as the last ranger climbed into the back of the lorry and the driver started the motor, the elephant moved and set off in pursuit.

Mulanye's release took place late in the afternoon. Not long after the rangers had returned to their station, the sun set. Half an hour later a large grey form moved silently through the shadows, lifted the latch on the gate and entered the deserted stockade. In the morning, when Godfrey went to clean out the pen, he found his friend standing quietly munching hay. She flapped her ears and ambled towards him, patting him with her trunk, rumbling her deep, contented rumble and obviously pleased to have rediscovered her friend. It was clear to everyone that the young elephant had no intention of leaving; the rangers were now her herd and Godfrey was her leader.

After a bit of patient teaching, Mulanye did learn to let Godfrey out of her sight. His duties as a ranger would have been very restricted if everywhere he went he had an elephant in tow. Once she had learned that he would always come back in the evening, Mulanye settled down and found other ways of amusing herself in his absence. Often these involved making a nuisance of herself around the ranger station, where others were trying to work, or where other animals were housed in pens. In the first six months, Godfrey had to sort out Mulanye's misbehaviour on many occasions. The true problem was that she really wanted to help but, unfortunately, kept getting the method wrong.

After the fourth or fifth incident and many arguments among the rangers, Godfrey decided to try and teach Mulanye to perform certain daily tasks that were necessary around the station. These involved moving bales of hay to pens where other sick animals were housed, replenishing water troughs and sweeping the yard in front of the station buildings. Mulanye was a quick learner and, because Godfrey made the tasks into a game, she joined in well. By the end of six months she had entirely taken over sweeping the yard and refilling the water troughs in each pen. She would also stand beside the fence near other sick animals as though keeping watch on them, while providing reassuring company.

This became clear when an antelope that had been brought in a week or so previously, suddenly started to have fits. Mulanye sought out the vet, where he was working elsewhere in the station and, holding him firmly by the hand, dragged him over to the pen that held the twitching antelope. As a result Ted was able to administer drugs and save its life.

"Befoah dis you are sweeper. Now you make it nurse for sick animal," Godfrey told his friend that evening. "You becamin very good park ranger, Mulanye. Tomorrow I ask him Missa Kernan give you propah job heeah, same like me!"

A few weeks later, a ten-year-old elephant cow was hit and killed by a mammy wagon while she crossed the road, hurrying to catch up with her herd. The six-month-old bull calf that was following behind suddenly became an orphan and was left standing by his mother's smashed body beside the road. The herd had been travelling at speed and the cow and her calf had been over a mile behind when the accident happened, so none of the others came back to look for them immediately. Maybe later, when the herd slowed, they would linger and look behind, waiting for their sister and her calf to catch up, but by then events had moved on and their sister was dead.

It was just luck that the next vehicle along that road was one of the park's own lorries, with three rangers on board. They had been out releasing some porcupines and were heading back to the ranger station. After checking that there was nothing to be done for the mother, the rangers used the lorry to drag its carcass clear of the road. Then they loaded up the confused calf and brought him with them, back to the station.

As the driver steered the truck into the stockaded pen, another ranger hopped down and went in search of Godfrey and his elephant. They needed no encouragement to come. Mulanye had heard a brief trumpet from the distressed calf and immediately pricked her ears. She headed straight over to the pen, lifted the latch and let herself in. By the time Godfrey had arrived she was running her trunk over the youngster and rumbling deep reassuring noises to calm him down.

"Now you muss be mammy elefant as well," Godfrey told her, and went to make up a bucket of powdered milk for the new inmate.

Mulanye was a natural at her new task and the calf soon settled down. It did not take him long to learn to trust Godfrey as well as she did and to allow him to do whatever he wanted. So Godfrey became the master of a second elephant, whom he named Peter. Three months later, another young cow, a little older than the bull calf, was added to the herd. Her mother had been killed by poachers and the calf had refused to follow the herd and be adopted by an aunt, despite obvious attempts by the older elephants to get her to go. In the end, the rangers had no alternative but to take this new orphan and entrust her to Mulanye and Godfrey's care. Godfrey named her Misu, because he said she was a pretty calf.

At the end of the year, when another injured elephant was

brought in, Robert Kernan decided that a new ranger station would have to be built, so that the elephants could have more room and also with a view to somehow engineering their return to the wild. The new elephant was a four-year-old female who had been shot several times in the shoulder, with arrows, and subsequently mauled by lions when she lagged behind her herd. Exactly why the lions had given up on what must have been easy prey was unclear, but a farmer had reported the incident and the rangers had collected the injured elephant. Once again, Mulanye was called upon to act as nursemaid and Peter and Misu shared the stockade with her. After a few days the new cow was named Alice.

When the new elephant camp was set up, John Ofonde was appointed to run it, with Godfrey as his assistant. It was situated at a place called Idindaba, some miles north-east of the original ranger station, beside a small tributary of the Red Volta River and beneath a grove of tall jacaranda trees, which gave it its name. The camp consisted of an accommodation block and mess hall, a store and an office, together with a small barn. There was also a stockaded animal pen and a couple of small pens with wire mesh fencing. The whole camp was surrounded by a tall chain-link wire fence with a belt of thorny bushes and cacti planted around the outside. There was a small water tower with a windmill on top of it to pump water up from the stream and an auxiliary diesel pump for those occasions when a greater volume of water was required.

Mr Kernan proposed to take the two rangers, all their gear and the four elephants to the new camp by truck, but Godfrey had other ideas. For some months before the move, he had been climbing up on Mulanye's shoulders and riding around the station. As they progressed, these rides took the pair further afield, sometimes several miles from the ranger station. Most of the time, wherever Mulanye went, she was accompanied by three other young elephants. Now Godfrey felt confident that he could steer her out into the more distant bush and that the other three would follow. If they ever hoped to persuade any of these elephants back to a wild life, this could be an important step. John Ofonde, together with the baggage and supplies, could go by road, but Godfrey was determined that he and his elephants would go on foot.

Few people have ever successfully trained African elephants to be ridden and there had always been a popular myth that it could not be done, because they had no history of being domesticated like Asiatic elephants. Godfrey had been studying hard and had read accounts of attempts by the colonial German army in East Africa, back in the late 1920s, to train elephants for riding and to carry military equipment. The Belgians had an elephant training school in the Congo which had marginal success with the small forest elephants, but Godfrey's herd was a different species entirely. He had also read about plains elephants being ridden in the great inland delta called Okavango, in southern Africa, so he saw no reason why his elephants should not also permit people to ride them. Mulanye already worked and performed regular housekeeping duties about the station and he wasn't going to let her or any other elephant hang around idly. If she wanted to stay, she had to pay for her keep. In the new camp the other three would all have to do something useful as well.

It was almost a year after the day when Godfrey had hurried to the ranger station to tell them about an injured elephant that the new camp was opened. During that time, as well as joining in with all the other ranger duties, Godfrey had become something of an expert on elephants. He had read everything he could find in print and had even written, with Ted's help, to game parks in other countries, with enquiries about how they managed their herds. He watched his four charges carefully and observed the wild herds in the reserve, making copious notes about their behaviour and preferences. He knew what plants they liked to graze and which they avoided. He knew which fruits they liked at different seasons and which plants they appeared to use as purgatives or for other 'medicinal' purposes.

The week before the move, Robert Kernan arrived with some interesting news. He had received a letter from a research laboratory in London where scientists had finally identified the sickness that had so nearly killed Mulanye. It was a virulent viral infection, for which there was no known treatment, and it affected only two African species: elephants and rock hyrax. It was invariably fatal and the laboratory knew of only one elephant previously to have survived, and that had been in a European zoo. They reported that during the previous recorded outbreaks, most of which had been in colonial Tanganyika and Nyasaland, the herds had always abandoned stricken animals, as if trying to prevent the disease from spreading to the rest of the herd. To Godfrey, this explained why Mulanye's herd had abandoned her.

Because he had stayed with her during the time she was most in need of support, Godfrey had become her herd leader. Now with the arrival of the three younger orphans, she was slowly becoming the leader of her own herd, despite still being so young herself. One day, he knew, she would be a true matriarch, and would probably have calves of her own.

OVER THE YEARS THAT followed, more orphan pachyderms were brought in by the rangers and they too became part of the herd. Each new arrival learned the skills that enabled them to integrate and still be left at liberty around the ranger station. One or two had had moments when they wreaked havoc and destroyed a barn or another light animal pen, but mostly they were a peaceful group who behaved themselves under the joint guidance of Godfrey and Mulanye.

Godfrey had been riding on Mulanye's shoulders ever since she recovered from the virus. Now he regularly rode her when he went out into the bush on his routine patrols. The rest of her small herd followed behind. As the years passed and other orphans grew big enough to be ridden, some of the other rangers also adopted this form of transport, but only when they were to accompany Godfrey, because their steeds, while happy enough to be ridden when with the herd, were most unwilling to leave their companions and venture off alone, even under the instructions of a ranger whom they had known and trusted since infancy.

For some reason Mulanye never grew significant tusks. She had short stubs, of course, but these protruded no more than a few inches beyond her lips. Whereas most of the wild females in the park who were of a similar age to Mulanye had tusks two to three feet long, hers never grew any bigger. Strangely none of the other orphans grew proper tusks either. Ivory poaching had never been a major problem in the game reserve but it was not unknown. This tuskless feature in Mulanye and her little herd proved to be a useful advantage since they would never be targeted by ivory poachers. On the few occasions when, like their wild cousins, they needed tusks, to dig up salt and mineral rich deposits or to gouge the pithy pulp from baobab trees, the herd's needs were met by Godfrey and the other rangers. Mulanye was adept at indicating precisely what deposits she wanted excavated.

This had the added benefit that Godfrey was able to collect accurate samples for analysis and, by watching how much each elephant consumed, make a scientific assessment of the animal's mineral intake. This was nutritional information that had previously been purely anecdotal.

Godfrey was sent away on a number of short courses to learn about the management of game and game parks. He read every book he could lay his hands on, particularly those about elephants, and not just those relating to African elephants. Without any great recognition, he acquired significant expertise in the study and care of elephants and, by the 1970s, undoubtedly understood in detail things which the more formal scientific community were only just beginning to discover. With the passage of years and all the experience he had gained, Godfrey rose steadily through the ranks of the Ghana Wildlife Service and became the deputy manager of the reserve.

Money was tight and the Ghana Wildlife Service was always under-funded. Like all the other reserves in the country, this northernmost park had to make do and mend for most things and depended on outside grants, won only after lengthy and tedious application processes through foreign agencies, for anything that was not routine. Even so the elephants in the reserve all flourished; so did the other animals.

IT WAS THE DROUGHT in early 1970 that first brought me to the area. Since much of my work was in some way related to water resources, it was not surprising, one day, to receive a request for help with water supplies in the northern game reserve. The letter requesting my assistance came from Godfrey and was posted in Bolgatanga. He outlined the existing resources and what he saw as the principal problems with great clarity and an economy of words that immediately intrigued me. His letter informed me that he had a good workforce at his disposal, which included a small herd of working elephants. This captured my imagination for working elephants were almost unheard of on this continent. The only time this had been achieved was in the 1940s with small forest elephants at a place called Gangala-na-Bodio in the Belgian Congo, up near the Ugandan border. But these were plains elephants and very much larger. I had to see this with my own eyes.

I made my first visit in early November 1970 on a dull, overcast day when the sticky air was thick with clouds of insects. Although this was no longer the rainy season, such weather was not uncommon and would continue for another month or so until the dry northerly wind from the Sahara came in December and drove the assembled clouds away towards the coast, leaving the land desiccated and covered in desert dust. Now the countryside was green, grass and leaves were plentiful and some of the fruiting trees still bore a little fruit. I should be seeing the park's water resources at their most abundant and its animals in peak condition.

The eye, however, can be deceptive. Although the countryside was green, it soon became apparent that the rains had been much less abundant than the land needed. For some years the annual rainfall had been declining and the parched lands of the sub-Saharan zone were creeping southwards. This year they had advanced again, but now with a more noticeable effect.

Much of the grass was already turning yellow. Most of the trees had finished fruiting and the animals and birds that depended on their fruit had stripped what remained, even before it was fully ripe. Even the baobabs, which should have been in leaf at this time of year, had been stripped of their greenery by hungry primates, both human and simian, in search of the minerals and vitamins which the leaves held. All that remained were the unripe pendulous fruits, suspended like huge olive Christmas tree baubles from the twisted, grey, root-like branches.

As I drove further into the park I began to appreciate why Godfrey had asked for help. The villages and small farms I passed on the outskirts had already cleared their fields. The grain had ripened early and produced only a meagre harvest and there was little joy and few offers of food in the places where I halted to ask directions. This alone was unusual, for the people hereabouts are normally most hospitable and press fruit, bread or millet beer on anyone who stops their vehicle.

I stopped in Nangodi to ask directions and found a man called Gulogo, who claimed to know where the Idindaba ranger station was located. He agreed, for a ridiculously small fee, to act as my guide. When I asked him what had happened to produce the despondency among his people, he shrugged and looked gloomy.

"Rain he be no good; harvest she be no good; ebrybody be hangry; nobody hab money for go anada place. All diss becos God be cross wid us."

Although I tried to get him to explain, he was unwilling to say any more, almost as if just talking about it would increase whatever offence had been committed and therefore make the punishment more severe. Amazingly he neither made any excuses nor asked for any sympathy. He simply accepted that he and his people had done something wrong and must endure God's punishment without complaint. In God's time they would be reprieved and things would improve again.

I decided to deliver a little of that reprieve immediately and told him that I expected to be in the game park for a week and needed someone to help me with my work. I would employ him for the week, at a good daily rate, if he would come with me to the game park. I told him also that I would feed him and pay him a bonus at the end if he had been helpful.

His face transformed at this news. "What you go do?"

"I have to meet a man called Godfrey Akempula at the Idindaba game ranger station, to look at water supplies in the park," I said.

"Dis wan elefant man?" he asked.

"Yes. Do you know him?"

"Dis man cousin my wife!" he announced with a grin. "Him very cleva man."

It was reassuring to know that the man I was due to meet was well reputed among the local community. We shook hands on the deal and Gulogo went off to tell his wife that he would be away for a few days. He came back half an hour later, with a *wawaga* over his shoulder which contained all he needed for a week away from home.

Gulogo turned out to be a good choice of guide, for he knew the countryside well. He was about fifty years old, and had a small farm outside the village. In his youth he had hunted through much of the region, before the game reserve became fully established, so he also knew where most of the best watering places were. He had finally given up hunting after being chased up a young kapok tree by an angry buffalo when he had been trying to shoot it with a bow and poisoned arrow. The buffalo had charged him with such a frightening turn of speed that he had scrambled up the nearest tree to escape, dropping his weapons as he did so. The enraged animal had spent more than an hour circling and ramming the tree trunk with its armour plated head, almost shaking Gulogo out of his precarious perch several times. His plight was made worse by the colony of red fire ants that inhabited the tree as these had attacked and swarmed over him, biting every part of his body until he felt raw all over. Unfortunately the buffalo was still patrolling below so he could not descend and run to the nearest water hole to relieve his agony.

Fortunately for Gulogo, the original incident had happened in the morning. In the midday heat the buffalo had finally given up trying to dislodge him from the tree and retired to seek shade and water for itself. Even then, Gulogo felt he had to wait at least an hour before climbing down. He knew that buffalo can be treacherous beasts and he was not entirely sure this one had really gone away. It might well have been hiding in a thicket, waiting for him to come down so that it could renew its attack.

When he finally got home, late that afternoon, Gulogo was in agony from all the ant bites. His hands and feet, as well as his arms and legs, were badly lacerated from holding on to the branches among the short sharp thorns with which his chosen refuge was thickly covered. His mother and aunts made salves from various leaves and the village medicine man gave him vile concoctions to drink, but their power to relieve his agony was not enough. He suffered terribly for a week or more before the pain subsided and it took many weeks for his skin to return to normal. Even then, it had a blotchy appearance that remained in perpetuity as a reminder of his adventure. Gulogo had never hunted again. He had also, he told me, never climbed another tree, even to collect fruit or honey.

None of the rangers were at the station when we reached Idindaba, but we knew we had come to the right place because the gate was blocked by an elephant who refused to move and just stood there flapping her ears and swinging her trunk from side to side. I tried hooting the horn, but was simply ignored. There seemed to be no way round this obstacle, so we just sat and waited. About twenty minutes later a small green pickup arrived, drove straight past us and up to the elephant. As though it had been waiting for this vehicle, the elephant immediately stepped sideways to let it enter the compound, then turned and followed it in. I restarted the motor and drove in, keeping a respectful distance behind just in case the elephant decided we should still not enter. Once inside, it ambled off to a patch of shade under one of the tall trees that dotted the compound. I turned the other way and parked next to the pickup where the driver was just emerging.

The man was smartly dressed in a ranger's uniform and he greeted us warmly. This was Assefe Musana, one of Godfrey's assistants, who apologised for his boss's absence. There was a court case involving a poacher who had been caught with a dead leopard. Godfrey had been obliged to go and give evidence against the man and would not be back before dark. Meanwhile, Assefe would take us round the station and its immediate surroundings and show us the park maps and water hole records.

I asked him about the elephant that had blocked the gate.

"That is Dodo," he laughed. "All other elefants have gone to the bush, to find food and to see their friends. But Dodo decided he is camp guard. When nobody is here he guards the gate to stop people from entering. He only moves for rangers or for park cars."

"It sounds like an ideal security system," I said.

"Oh, yes. It's very safe here," Assefe laughed. "Dodo controls the gate and we have Johnny inside." He pointed to the tree under which the elephant had sought shade. A large male lion was lying there, watching us intently. This was indeed an interesting security system and a place where it would be unwise for any stranger to wander round uninvited.

Assefe was enjoying my surprise and when I looked at him again he explained: "Johnny's an old boy now; he can't move fast with his bad foot. But people are still afraid of his big teeth." Later Godfrey explained, as he ran his fingers through the lion's mane, that Johnny had been found as a small cub with one hind foot caught in a gin trap. It must have happened several days before he was found for the wound was badly infected and the bones were severely broken. The park vet had done his best, but part of the foot had been lost. With his usual style, Godfrey had simply adopted the injured cub, trained it to behave properly and given it a home and a job at the ranger station. Like all his other staff, Johnny earned his keep. He was the camp watchman.

I thought this was a novel way of saving on the wage bill.

Godfrey arrived back after dark, a short stocky man, with a huge smile and an easy manner. He now spoke excellent English as well as French, which he had learned because the park now spanned the border and was jointly controlled by the Ghanaian and Haute Volta wildlife authorities. The latter was more a formality than any real control, because Haute Volta was, in those days, the poorest country in the world and could not afford to spend money on things like game reserves. Even so, Godfrey ensured that his staff were recruited from both sides of the border.

When he saw Gulogo, Godfrey was delighted. The two spent several minutes catching up on family news before Godfrey turned back to me. "You couldn't have chosen a better man to bring with you," he informed me. "This man has quite a reputation as a water diviner. If you want to find any underground water in this area, he is the person to ask."

It seemed my visit was off to a good start, and I was pleased to have found a man with such talents. Maybe I could use his skills in other places as well.

The following morning Godfrey took us on a tour of the reserve's principal watering holes and showed us the main rivers and streams that flowed through. This park covered most of the upper reaches of the White and Red Volta rivers. It was alarming to see how low they were. On previous visits to these rivers I had noted more than double the present flow. A lot of the other streams that normally flowed across the reserve were dry or empty channels with occasional muddy pools in them. This meant the animals had fewer watering points to choose from and consequently the surrounding areas were being badly over-grazed.

While the carnivores in the park had found hunting much easier, because of the concentrations of grazers near the waterholes and rivers, other animals were not doing so well. Godfrey and his team had even given some consideration to a structured cull to reduce numbers to the level the land could support. The need for this was made more pressing because some herds of grazers had moved south, beyond the reserve's boundary, in search of better grazing and more plentiful water. The farmers whose land they invaded were already feeling the effects of the drought through decreased crop yields so this shift by the wild herds provoked a hostile response.

Looking at the park maps, I had seen several areas that appeared to have no natural water and I wondered about these. Godfrey told me that some of them were the locations of large rock outcrops, but one or two were simply empty grassland or, in the present drought, bare ground. We decided to go and look at some of these and I asked Gulogo to see if there was any underground water to be found. In one place he found a strong indication and told me that the water would not be more than the height of three men down.

Godfrey, who only stood about five-foot-four, and I, a foot taller, looked at one another and both burst out laughing.

"What size man?" I asked.

"Man high like me," Gulogo said, slightly petulantly. "You be too long; him too short. Propah man height like me!" He too joined in the laughter. We put a marker in the ground and resolved to come back later in the week and sink a test bore with the equipment that was sitting in my Land Rover, back at the ranger station.

On the way back I asked Godfrey about his elephants and he told me the long tale of Mulanye and the others and how he had come to be a game ranger. As we neared Idindaba, he stopped the pickup and pointed off into the bush.

"There she is," he said, waving towards some scrubby trees.

For several moments I could see nothing but open bush, but then something moved. A moment later I could see a dozen large grey forms emerging from the scrub. Godfrey tooted the horn and the herd immediately veered towards us. A minute later the vehicle was surrounded by huge grey bodies, rumbling deep in their bellies as their trunks explored the vehicle and its occupants. I was caught unawares by one soft trunk that came through the open window on the passenger side as I was looking the other way. Something soft and velvety brushed my ear and began to tickle the back of my neck.

"Just sit still," Godfrey said, quietly. "You are perfectly safe. They just want to know who you are."

After perhaps five minutes, when each of the elephants had

made its inspection, the animals moved away from the vehicle and Godfrey restarted the engine. We drove off slowly with the herd following behind. After a hundred yards, Godfrey accelerated and we left them behind.

"They'll come back to the camp now," he told us. "When they know there are strangers about they are the most inquisitive animals I know. They'll want to come and have another look at you and also inspect your Land Rover. After that, they will know you."

Twenty minutes after we arrived back at the ranger station the herd arrived. There were eleven of them and Godfrey introduced each one and asked us to shake hands, or rather to shake trunks. Mulanye was now a magnificent beast, standing over six feet tall at the shoulder. The old wound still showed as a broad diagonal stripe down her right flank and her gait was very slightly uneven where her hind leg had been broken all those years ago. She was also very much the boss. If one lingered too long over the introductions she delivered a smart whack with a leafy branch held in her trunk, pushing it away to let the next come forward.

Having inspected us, the elephants turned their attention to my vehicle and gave that a good once-over, even pushing aside the canvas cover over the tailgate to explore the equipment in the back with their trunks.

It all seemed surreal; everything I had heard about Godfrey and his elephants was true and I found it amazing to be surrounded by these huge wild animals and yet feel so safe. Even Johnny the lion seemed as tame as a domestic moggy, although I didn't get too close to him. The elephants, I noted, all passed nearby, stretching out their trunks towards him as they arrived in the camp, as if to clock in with the watchman.

For the rest of that first afternoon I listened as Godfrey explained how the park was managed, how many of each species it held and how their food and watering needs were being managed. He had long wanted to build small dams on a few of the Volta tributaries, but the water authorities had consistently refused him permission without even bothering to visit the area. He was frustrated and wanted to create some decent new water storage to see his herds through what he expected were going to be increasingly dry years ahead.

This was only a small park, even though its size had been increased to cross the border. It was now about the size of Wiltshire. While the game population was reasonably high, the place was not teeming with animals like some of the big parks in East Africa. Even so, a balance had to be maintained and it was perhaps more difficult in this park than in parks as big as small countries that existed elsewhere. Godfrey and his team had their strategy worked out. Now they needed to get the water question sorted.

Godfrey had further court commitments for the following day, so I decided that Gulogo and I would go out and put down a few test bores in those places where Gulogo's dowsing had detected aquifers. In any case, after listening to all Godfrey's plans for an afternoon and an evening, I had a lot to think about. As we climbed into the Land Rover the next morning, Godfrey was about to set off to court and was giving his rangers their last instructions for the day. It was incongruous to see a smart parade of rangers backed by a line of elephants who appeared also to be part of the parade. So they were, for when Godfrey had finished instructing the rangers he turned to the elephants and gave them instructions as well.

"This place is a mess," he told the pachyderm patrol. "You have been lazy and not swept the compound. When I come back I want to see it smart. There is also debris lying outside the fence. You can clear that as well. Then you can go out to the bush and play."

I could swear the elephants nodded in acknowledgement.

"And Dodo," he singled out the one that had blocked the gate the day before. "When these men come back," he pointed to Gulogo and me, "you must let them enter. Now, everybody go to work."

The parade dispersed and Gulogo and I climbed into the Land Rover and went about our business. It was a half-hour drive to the site where I proposed to sink the first test bore. On the way there I explained to Gulogo what we were going to do. He was a quick learner and as soon as we had the equipment out of the vehicle and I had shown him how it went together, I could see that he understood precisely how the narrow coring drill worked. We bored eight holes that day and a further six the following day. On the second day, as we were cleaning out the cores after the last but one test hole, Godfrey arrived with his herd and one of the younger rangers.

The two men climbed down to talk to us and Godfrey told Mulanye to take the herd back to the station; he would return with us in the Land Rover. To my astonishment, the elephants wheeled round and departed in the direction from which they had come.

"You get used to it," Godfrey told me. "They are like children really. They know that if they are good, and go straight back, there will be a piece of sugar cane for each of them when I return."

"Don't you have any children, then?" I asked, not sure whether or not Godfrey even had a wife.

"No. I have not yet found a wife who can put up with my animals," he explained. "All the girls that I know think I am bewitched by some magic spirit, so they are reluctant to be alone with me. That makes finding a wife very difficult in our traditional society. Anyway, I have enough to worry about with the animals. I don't need nagging as well." He laughed and threw up his hands in a gesture of easy acceptance.

We turned our attention back to the results of the survey, for I had found something interesting that might offer a novel and cheap way of storing water in one particular spot, close to one of the roads that crossed the park. The road in question was almost straight for over a mile, with a distinct dip at the mid point. It was over fifteen feet wide and, although only a dirt road, it was made of good stable soil. An inch of rain falling on this stretch of road would deliver over seventy-eight thousand gallons of water, if it could be captured and stored.

Godfrey looked very interested as I explained this. He was even more interested when I revealed how it could be done. One of our test drillings had been close to this road, at the lowest point. Nine feet down, the core drill had started bringing up thick clay. The clay layer continued downwards for a further eleven feet. We would put down five or six more test drills the next day to confirm the extent of the clay, but it looked as if there was enough down there to line a very sizeable tank. If the ditches either side of the road could be directed to drain into the tank, there could be plenty of water.

"But the rainfall here is over eight inches per year," Godfrey pointed out, when I showed him the calculation, "Even though it has been decreasing each year."

"Then build a bigger tank, or more than one tank."

"How many roads can we do this on?" he asked, with growing excitement.

"You can do it wherever the ground profile and soil conditions permit, "I said, "Provided there is good clay to line the tank and stop the water seeping away."

Godfrey's face took on the ecstatic expression of Mr Toad dreaming of motor cars, and I almost expected to hear him say "Poop poop!"

The next morning Gulogo and I sank six more test bores to explore the extent and depth of the clay layer. We then marked out an area, about two hundred yards from the road, that might be suitable for a storage tank. There was plenty of clay available to ensure that the whole tank could be well lined with a waterproof layer. There was plenty of space for the tank and for animals to congregate around it, and the lie of the land most definitely lent itself to the proposed construction. The only problem that I could see was going to be that of getting the hole dug.

Godfrey did not think this was so much of a problem. He would deploy his park workforce with picks to loosen the soil and, he said, the elephants could help drag it out of the hole with some sort of plough or in carts. I had no idea what he meant, but having seen how resourceful this remarkable man could be, I had no doubt he would make light of the problem. Digging such a vast hole by hand, however, seemed to me to be a long term project.

I drew him a plan and some drawings to show how I envisaged the construction should proceed and how to use the excavated soil to build banks and channels that would direct the water from the roadside ditches into the tank. I also showed him where it would be necessary to put a culvert under the road so that water from the ditches on the other side could also be directed into the tank.

The following day, we left the game park; Gulogo to return to his wife in Nangodi, I to head west to visit projects in Côte d'Ivoire and southern Mali. Before dropping him off, I told Gulogo that I would employ him again the next time I came up to the park. He also agreed to come further north with me, into Mali, to offer some advice on water divining to students at the well digging school that had recently been launched.

IT WAS NINE WEEKS BEFORE I could get back and that time I saw some significant developments. Godfrey had persuaded the highways authorities to come and grade his roads and to reshape the ditches on either side of them. He had also managed to persuade the contract manager to leave one of his bulldozers at the place where the tank was to be dug, with the intention that he might be able to bribe the driver into excavating the hole for him. He was partially successful in this, but the bulldozer had broken down and the mechanics who came out to fix it insisted on taking it away on a low loader to be mended in their workshop.

When I returned to the park, the hole for the tank was less than half dug and there were huge piles of red earth all over the place. Something drastic needed to be done for, even with Godfrey's elephants helping to clear the loose soil, there was far too much earth still to move and the spring rains were only three months off. The elephants were still quite new to this type of work, so progress with them was slow and at times they were probably more of a hindrance than a help. I remembered that during a visit to Kumasi at the beginning of the year, I had seen a fleet of bulldozers in a government stock yard and wondered if one of them could be used.

I headed south, taking Gulogo with me, not because he was

needed, but because it would put some wages in his pocket and it would give me time to explain to him what was happening at the Mali wells school, and to explain what I wanted him to do there, when we went north again. He was also good company and had hidden talents.

The official in charge of the government storage yard at Kumasi was a charming fellow who agreed, over a good meal, that I could have any of the bulldozers I wanted. The problem was that they were all broken. These machines were actually petrol powered snow ploughs, donated, some years before, by the Soviet government as part of a huge aid package. They all had heavily insulated cabs, through which the engine exhaust ran to keep the driver warm in the frozen northern winters. They also had huge five-metre-wide, double snow plough blades that pushed the snow off to both sides. Every single machine had failed for want of a small electrical switch, so they had simply been pushed into the yard and abandoned.

It took me two hours to find a competent mechanic and a further three hours for him to diagnose the problem. He promised to have the parts and to mend one machine by lunch time the next day. That evening, I set Gulogo the task of finding a lorry big enough to carry one of these monsters north to the game park. I spent the evening using the hotel telex to obtain authorisation to draw enough funds to pay for this crazy project. In the morning I took this authorisation round to the bank and drew a fat wad of cash, amounting to over £2,000.

When I arrived at the yard the next morning, the haggling started and by midday the deals were all done. The mechanic had been as good as his word and soon had the machine running. He rapidly discovered that the driver would die of heat, because of the exhaust being directed through the cab, and obligingly removed the heavy armoured glass panels from all the cab's windows. It was only when we were loading it onto the lorry that Gulogo found a small lever which, when pulled, diverted the exhaust through a separate pipe that vented straight up from the engine housing without going anywhere near the cab. He immediately went in search of the glass panels, saying he could use them in his house. His wife would be very proud to have the only glass windowed house in Nangodi.

I purchased the Soviet snow plough, outright, for £200 in Godfrey's name. The mechanic charged me £30 for getting it running and for loading it onto the lorry that Gulogo had found. The lorry driver, who also happened to be its owner (and a friend of Gulogo's brother's wife's second cousin), charged me £150 for hauling the huge red monster north to the game park, and I bought £50 worth of fuel for it, not knowing how much petrol it would consume, but assuming that it would be thirsty. Four drums we loaded into the back of my Land Rover, just in case somebody thought to help himself if they travelled north on the lorry and the other two were wrapped in canvas and tied down behind the snow plough blade. I needn't have worried, as the driver had brought along three of his sons, all armed with sharp spears and bows with wickedly barbed and poisoned arrows, to act as guards.

It took three days to get the snow plough north to the game park. Godfrey and the other rangers were very excited when they saw it and even more so to discover that it now belonged to their park. Gulogo had taken lessons from the mechanic and was now a passable, if basic, driver. With a bit more practice he could be good and Godfrey was open to the idea of employing him whenever he needed to use the machine in the future.

The snow plough blade was far from ideal, but it did enable us to dig out and shift most of the earth that had to be removed from the tank. It was, however, very good at shaving the clay layer, when we got down to it, so that large slabs, nine inches thick, could be laid on the sloping sides of the tank and tramped down by elephants' feet, to form a more or less waterproof lining.

As the tank was nearing completion we made another interesting discovery. Walking around in the bottom of the tank, when we stopped work at midday, Gulogo picked up some long sticks that had been blown in by the wind. Holding these, one in each hand, he felt an immediate reaction from the sticks. He repositioned his hands and took a firmer hold, as if searching for an aquifer. Again the sticks started pulling downwards and he called me over.

"Big water here," he told me. "You must make a hole and suck him out. Water will stop clay from breaking before rain comes to fill the tank."

I could see immediately what he meant, for I had been wondering how we would stop the clay from shrinking and keep the tank watertight until the rains came. Just off to the side of the tank we set up the test rig and started drilling. It was only capable of going down to about fifty feet, but Gulogo was certain there was good water just below the clay. It had not shown up so strongly before because of the depth of the clay, but in the tank we had now shaved that down to less than half its original depth, so Gulogo's wands had felt its pull.

Sure enough, at forty-three feet, the one-inch test drill hit water. We cleaned out the core and put down a narrow pipe, attaching a suction pump to the top and were rewarded with a steady flow of good water that soon cleared.

"We need a proper borehole and a wind pump," I told Godfrey.

"There is a disused windmill at an abandoned ranger station at the other end of the park," he told me. "I don't know if there is a pump."

The lorry that had brought the snow plough up was about to head back south, but a small financial incentive persuaded the driver to take his lorry over to the abandoned station and fetch the windmill. One of the rangers would show him the way. Godfrey promised to be there in the morning with lifting gear to dismantle the windmill and load the lorry. The driver, unsuspecting, accepted this as normal and set off happily but, by the look in Godfrey's eye, I suspected that the driver was in for a surprise in the morning.

A surprise was just what he got, for Godfrey arrived early, riding on Mulanye's shoulders, with three other rangers similarly mounted. The lorry driver ran, terrified, to his cab, where he locked himself in and peered anxiously out as his lorry was surrounded by the huge grey beasts. Godfrey ignored him and got on with the task of dismantling the windmill. The blades and wind vane were swiftly unbolted and the securing bolts that held the pump shaft together and others that fixed the pylon to its base were removed. Then, with some of the elephants holding ropes, while others held on to the pylon, it was lowered gently to the horizontal.

It took only two elephants to pick up the pylon and lay it on the flat bed of the truck. Within an hour all the other parts of the windmill and its pump were tied down and the driver could start back. Unfortunately he was still locked in his cab, hiding down among the pedals under the steering wheel. He would not come out and unlock the cab until there were no elephants to be seen.

Eventually the driver emerged and was persuaded, for another small financial consideration, to drive back to the tank. From there I took him, in my Land Rover, down to Nangodi and then back to the Idindaba ranger station, where we waited until Godfrey arrived to say that the lorry had been unloaded and the elephants had gone into the bush to play. The driver set off south without delay, no doubt to spread lurid tales about how he had escaped from rampaging wild beasts by the skin of his teeth.

Godfrey and his team soon built a new base for the windmill, above the one-inch bore we had left in place. When the pylon was erected a few days later, once again with the assistance of Mulanye and her herd, we pulled out the one-inch pipe and used the pylon as a drilling tower to help sink a four-inch tube.

Within a week the windmill was working, pumping out a steady flow of clean water that was then sprayed all over the tank to prevent the clay lining from drying out before the rains came. One of the rangers was detailed to keep Mulanye and her herd away from the tank.

SOON AFTER THAT GULOGO and I went north into Haute Volta and from there onwards to Mali. The rains had begun by the time we came back and when we arrived at the Idindaba station the place looked green and lush; the big flame tree that provided shade over the middle of the compound was beginning to flower. The rangers were very excited because of the rain and wanted to take us immediately to Lake Mulanye.

This was the name they had given the tank once it began to fill with water. The name was given, not only because of the help that the elephants had provided during construction, but because, since it began to fill with water, it had been almost impossible to get the herd away from the place.

"What are you worrying about?" I asked Godfrey, when he told me this news. "You were trying to find some way of getting her and the others back to the wild. It sounds as though this has done it."

"In a way, yes," he said, with a big sigh. "But they will keep stopping the traffic that passes down the road and they are becoming a nuisance. They hang around the tank all the time, turning it into a wallow, and then spray fountains of dirty water at anyone who stops to look at them, as if they think this is funny! It is damaging our tourist trade and we have people coming to complain almost every day. They are also preventing any of the other animals from getting at the water. While he was out on patrol last week, Gonme saw them drive off a herd of Zebra that had come to drink."

We spent hours discussing the problem, but no immediate solution presented itself. Finally I suggested we should go to the site and have a look. As we approached the top of the incline on the road leading down to the tank, Godfrey asked me to stop. He suggested we should approach on foot as this was less likely to warn the herd of our presence and we would be able to see their behaviour.

Sure enough, the elephants were all there, using the tank as a play pool; wallowing in the shallow water near the ramps leading down into it, rolling about and spraying themselves and one another with the brown soupy water. Only two animals were not in the water; they stood on the bank watching, as if on guard. As we watched, from behind a bush a hundred and fifty yards from the tank, a pair of bucks emerged from the scrub, obviously looking for a drink. The sentinels immediately turned to face them, flapping their ears and lifting trunks in warning and the bucks retired, disappointed and still thirsty.

"The only thing to do is to make this unattractive as a wallow," I suggested. "Perhaps we should dig another tank somewhere else for the elephants and reduce this one to just a drinking hole."

"That sounds fine," said Godfrey, "but how?"

"Fill the whole thing with huge rocks and leave only a small space at one end with free water visible. The water will still fill the spaces between the rocks, and it may help reduce evaporation, but the elephants won't be able to get in."

While we talked about this idea, a tourist car came down the road from the other direction. We saw it slow down as the occupants saw the elephants and then stop where the road was nearest to the tank. We could hear the excited voices of the tourists, speaking German, as they pushed their camera lenses out of the open windows. One of the sentries put her trunk down into the water and took a long draught. Then she turned and walked away into the nearby scrub. The tourists were enthralled by the animals in the water and took no notice.

After a few moments the driver of the car opened his door and climbed out with a large camera. He moved a few feet from the car to get a better angle from which to take what promised to be a Pulitzer Prize winning picture. As he lifted the camera to take the shot, the sentry, who turned out to be Misu, emerged quietly from the bushes behind him, raised her trunk and doused him in five gallons of thick muddy water.

I doubled up with laughter, but Godfrey was outraged. Leaping to his feet, he charged forward, shouting at Misu and telling the tourist to get back in his car and drive to the top of the slope. As the man moved to comply, Godfrey stood there, just a couple of feet in front of the huge beast, wagging his finger at her and loudly telling her off for her antisocial behaviour. The elephant really did look sheepish and, if only I had been carrying a camera, that would surely have been the photo of a lifetime.

Having told off the elephant, Godfrey turned his attention to the tourist, who was still parked, gawping. He told him off equally forcefully, reminding him that the animals in the reserve were all wild and could be extremely dangerous. The effect of the moment was completely spoiled by Misu, who chose that moment to lay her trunk on Godfrey's shoulder and start tickling his ear.

That evening, back at Idindaba, we studied the park maps in search of a site for a new tank. We found two possible places and went out the next morning to inspect them. One, which lay about eight miles form the present tank, was ideal. There was a large rock outcrop sticking out of a gently sloping piece of ground and the landscape held a number of large trees that offered good shade. We staked out the tank site and put lines of pegs where collecting channels would be dug. At Godfrey's suggestion we also staked out a spot for a second, smaller tank, nearby that would be elephant-proofed with rocks and would provide a drinking spot for other animals. It would be a shame to collect all that run-off and not make best use of it.

Godfrey had found a mechanic with a welding torch who modified the blade on the snow plough to make it more effective as a bulldozer, so work should proceed apace. I took his fuel drums down to Bolgatanga and filled them for him before I left once more to attend to other projects. Gulogo stayed to drive the bulldozer.

The new tank took Godfrey and his team six weeks to build. They had to import clay from another deposit for the lining as there was none beneath the new site. The second, smaller, tank was dug half a mile away, round the other side of the rock outcrop. It was surrounded with large boulders to make access less easy for the elephants, but to permit other animals still to come and drink. Gulogo's brother's wife's second cousin came back from Kumasi with his lorry and helped transport huge rocks that were rolled into the original pit. While these reduced the tank's total capacity, the windmill pump still brought up water and was able to maintain a big enough pool for animals to drink.

Godfrey's elephants spent more and more of their time at the new Lake Mulanye and less of it hanging around the ranger station. Godfrey even had to hire a lad to keep the yard swept as their domestic duties lapsed. Although still quite tame, the herd had, effectively, been returned to the wild and now lived alongside the other two herds in the reserve.

IT WOULD BE NICE IF THIS was the happy conclusion to the tale of Godfrey's elephants, but sadly it did not turn out that way. There had been a revolution in Ghana and the government of Dr Busia was replaced by a military regime under Colonel Acheampong. Some newly empowered soldier, whose trade, after all, was about the use of guns, took it into his head to make a bit of extra money by granting big game hunting licences for rich tourists. Mulanye and her little herd were easy targets and soon fell as trophies. When Godfrey went to protest, he was summarily arrested and thrown into prison. In a short time he too was dead; like his beloved Mulanye, he caught an obscure virus but in his case there was no one to treat him. Two of his rangers were killed by trigger-happy tourists and the others faded into the bush whenever outsiders appeared. Johnny, the sentinel lion at Idindaba, died peacefully in his sleep at the age of nine and was buried in the compound, beneath his favourite tree. Not long after Godfrey's death, the remaining rangers abandoned Idindaba.

Today all that remains of Godfrey and his elephants is a large stone next to the second tank; carved into it in rough letters is 'Lake Mulanye'.

Mulanye and her herd in the bush near the ranger station.

Walkabout: On his 1963 visit to the Nigerian Army Training Depot at Zaria, General Mobutu (centre) is flanked on the left by school headmaster Major Peter Wakeman and Captain Avumbu, Mobutu's ADC, and on the right by Captain Damian Kisani, Nigerian Army liaison officer and the author's father, Colonel Richard Mathie, commander of the Nigerian Army Training Depot.

7 ~ An ordinary despot

A SMALL GROUP OF MEN walked across the scorching tarmac in the mid-morning sun and stopped at the foot of the aircraft's boarding steps. The visiting General turned to a smart young Nigerian official, who was dressed in brilliant white robes and a colourful embroidered hat, offering his hand to say his goodbyes. A fifteen-year-old European boy, looking slightly out of place in this august group, translated the General's words and the reply.

The General turned to the other military member of the party, a tall European man resplendent in the uniform of a Highland regiment and wearing a Colonel's insignia. After shaking hands he received a smart salute from this officer, who had been his host during the visit. He smiled, returning the salute before thanking the Colonel profusely, not only for the hospitality he and his wife had received in the Colonel's home, but also for the invaluable insights that his tour of the country's primary military training station had given him. The boy remained silent this time, as the Colonel spoke just enough French to understand the General's thanks and to offer his own farewell and good wishes for a safe flight.

With the formalities concluded, the two soldiers faced one

another again and exchanged smart salutes before the General turned to climb the steps. As he put his foot on the first step, he paused, turned back and addressed the boy.

"Thank you for your service. It has been very helpful to my mission here. How much have they paid you for your work?"

"Thirty pounds, sir," was the reply.

"You are worth much more than that!" the General said and, reaching into his breast pocket, withdrew a bundle of notes which he thrust into the boy's hand. "This is my thanks for your service," he said, "and I give you my personal invitation that if you ever come to my country, you must come and visit me in my home."

"Thank you sir, I shall remember that."

"I shall expect you," said the General. He shook the boy's hand, turned and climbed the steps. His wife, who had preceded him to the aircraft's door, met him at the top of the stairs. They waved to the small party on the apron below before disappearing inside.

The aircraft's door closed, the propellers spun and the four engines in turn coughed, belched clouds of smoke and growled into life before settling down to a throaty rumble. Moments later, the shiny military transport moved off and rumbled along the taxiway to the end of the runway. As the engines roared and the plane began to roll, a man seated on a camel, outside the airport's terminal building, raised a huge traditional trumpet to his lips and blew a long, drawn-out note that echoed mournfully over the sweltering airfield until the roar of the departing plane drowned it.

So ended the visit in 1963 of Lieutenant General Joseph-Désiré Mobutu, commander in chief of the Congolese army, to Northern Nigeria.

The man in white robes was Alhaji Ali Akilu, the newly

appointed Nigerian provincial governor, who had taken up his post only a couple of weeks earlier. Fortunately the purpose of the General's visit had been military, so his presence was merely a gesture of protocol and recognition that the Nigerian government had sanctioned the visit. This was necessary because the Colonel, who had been General Mobutu's real host, was – as his uniform implied – British. He had been in command of the recruitment and training depot for the whole Nigerian army since just before independence in 1960 and was due to hand over to a Nigerian commander the following year. He was also my father.

The third member of the farewell party, the boy, was me.

I should have been in school in England but had landed myself in a bit of trouble and had been sent home early for the Easter holidays. As a penance for my misdemeanours, my father decided I needed to do something useful to earn my keep, so I was co-opted to serve as interpreter for the General's visit.

My father spoke a little French and could understand a bit more, but not to the standard required for technical discussions about military recruitment and training. My proficiency in both French and English was adequate, plus I had the ability to switch from one to the other without losing track of what was going on. As a soldier's son, I had grown up in a military environment. I knew my way around the depot and was familiar with what went on there from the many times Dad and I had ridden around the place on horseback in the early evening to enable him to meet the troops informally and see the extracurricular activities like sports teams in action. As a result, the task seemed relatively straightforward. So Dad had conscripted me.

General Mobutu spoke very good French, although he used one or two odd expressions I had never come across before; I later realised he spoke an African version of Belgian French. This was to be expected since he was head of the army in what had, until recently, been the Belgian Congo. He was not a highly educated man, being reputedly only moderately literate, but he was a well-trained soldier with an astute grasp of all things military and political. He was also a very quick learner with an agile mind, and was quick to understand and appreciate the merits of the Nigerian Army training system. And he obviously knew how to lead men.

As my father and I walked back to the waiting military staff car, my father remarked, "That man has the seeds of greatness in him, but I'm not sure he will ever be an easy man to deal with." How prophetic those words were to be.

A DECADE LATER, AT TEN past eleven one sultry morning, I stepped from the cool air-conditioned interior of an Air Zaïre Boeing 707 into the steamy tropical heat of Kinshasa airport. It was like walking from a fridge into an exotically scented sauna. Within minutes my clothing was clinging and damp. The scent of this sauna may have been exotic, but that didn't mean it was pleasant. The whole place smelled of rank, rotting vegetation, overripe fruit and the unmistakable aroma of termites, which is not dissimilar to that of a public urinal on the Bognor Regis seafront on a hot summer afternoon. By the time I and the other hundred and forty passengers had walked the three hundred metres from where the aircraft stood to the terminal's arrivals doorway, we were wet through. The grey clouds chose that moment to release their burden in a heavy rain shower.

The officials in the arrivals hall were remarkably efficient and we were all through immigration and into the customs hall in less than half an hour. Here we had a longer wait, as the tractor towing the baggage trolleys had been swamped by the rain and was now inoperable. The baggage handlers were unable to bring our luggage in from the plane, so it sat on a train of trolleys while mechanics scratched their heads. Eventually another vehicle was found and our sodden luggage was driven into the hall, off-loaded and lined up along the customs bench.

We passengers, meanwhile, had been herded behind a rope barrier and kept there until all the bags were accounted for. We were then called forward in turn, by a man with a passenger list on his clip-board, who asked us to identify our baggage. As soon as each person had done so, a porter was waved forward to carry it to another bench at the far end of the hall, behind which stood an army of customs officers. The passenger was required to pay the porter for his service, in foreign currency only, not the local zaïres, before the customs officers would begin their examination.

Predictably, the customs inspection involved opening every bag and suitcase and emptying the entire contents onto the bench, to be rifled through by at least three people. Anything that was considered suspect, or possibly just caught the customs officer's fancy, was confiscated without appeal. The rest was dumped unceremoniously back into the suitcase for the hapless passenger to repack. Sometimes, just as the case was being closed, another customs officer would come along and insist on inspecting the whole lot again, usually confiscating something else.

The passenger had no choice but to tolerate this for any argument resulted in an instant fine of $100, payable in foreign currency, and removal to a private room for interrogation and further rifling through one's baggage. I was warned of this by another passenger who had been here before and suffered this fate, so I bit my tongue and said nothing. After all, this sort of behaviour was not uncommon in Africa in those days.

Happily, my turn came quite early, but it was still more than two hours after the plane had landed before I emerged from the terminal, accompanied by yet another porter who also required payment in foreign currency. There a wall of enthusiastic, shouting taxi drivers awaited, all trying to entice new arrivals to use their particular cab.

The porter deposited my bag on the ground so I could stand on top of it. As I towered above them, the milling crowd quietened enough for me to make myself heard as I demanded the price for a ride into town. I had been warned not to pay more than five zaïres and realised this was going to be a bit of a Dutch auction when most of the drivers demanded at least five times that amount. I singled out three drivers and started haggling with them. It took fifteen minutes to negotiate a sensible price, during which I remained firmly atop my suitcase to stop anyone seizing hold and carrying it off to his cab as a means of forcing me to accept his offer. Even so, I still had to step on several sets of fingers to stop them trying this ploy.

My porter, who was waiting patiently, carried the suitcase triumphantly towards the waiting vehicle where he stuffed it into the back seat beside me. I offered him a French ten-franc note for his services, which he accepted with a broad smile and much muttering of "*Merci, merci.*" I was a little surprised that he then climbed into the front seat of the taxi, beside the driver, and accompanied us into town. Just hitching a ride, I wondered, or perhaps I had bought his services all the way to my hotel.

So it proved to be, for when we arrived at the hotel he leapt out, dragged my suitcase out and delivered it to one of the hotel's own porters, saying *"Pas voleur!"* to me as he did so. I thought this was exceptional service, so I gave him another five francs, even though he was neither asking for or expecting it. This, of course, resulted in another chorus of *"Merci, merci monsieur. Beaucoup merci!"* The taxi driver was similarly friendly as I paid him off and added a small tip. Then I followed the hotel porter inside and approached the reception desk.

Word had somehow preceded me, for they knew who I was even before I told them. The two clerks were efficiency itself, checking me in, handing my key to the porter and assuring me that my baggage would be safely delivered to the room, and then providing me with local currency at the publicly declared exchange rate and filling in all the forms that this required. The clerk told me to keep the forms safe, as the amount of foreign currency I had brought with me had been recorded at the airport and I would be in trouble with the government if I failed to record all my subsequent exchanges.

After lunch I approached the reception desk to ask how a visitor should go about presenting his credentials at the President's office. My enquiry was overheard by two large men in crisp military uniforms who were standing at the desk talking to the other clerk. They both wore shiny black boots and belts, black berets sporting very colourful cap badges, and wrap-around mirror sunglasses. In fact they looked like a pair of Grahame Greene's Tonton Macoutes. They behaved like them too, for in moments there was one either side of me and they were asking why I wanted to know about the President's office.

"Because many years ago, before he became President, I met him," I replied. "And he told me that if ever I came to his country I should visit him. I merely wanted to leave my card at his office, as a courtesy, to let him know that I am here and have not forgotten."

"Monsieur Mathie, the President already knows you are here. You are to come with us," one of them said. Together, they propelled me through the front door and into a waiting black Mercedes, which sped off into the chaotic traffic of central Kinshasa as soon as the doors were closed. The vehicle, although apparently unmarked, was obviously easily identifiable to the traffic police who manned every intersection, for they held up other vehicles to wave us through. As a result it took less than fifteen minutes to travel the length of the Avenue 30 Juin and reach the presidential compound.

As we drove in through the side gate, I was thinking about the colleagues I had been expecting to meet that afternoon. Most of them had arrived a week before me; they were to pick me up from the hotel at three o'clock. Now they would arrive to find that I had been snatched by two policemen and hustled off to some unspecified destination. It was bound to give at least a couple of them, who were twitchy at the best of times, a bit of a scare as there had been a number of stories going the rounds about westerners who had disappeared without explanation in this country. Now one of their own colleagues had vanished.

These thoughts came to a halt as the car pulled up in front of a doorway. A liveried attendant opened the car door and ushered me towards the entrance, where I was met by a smartly dressed young man who said he was one of the Presidential secretaries and invited me to follow him along a broad and richly furnished corridor. Around a few corners and across an open hallway, I was ushered through tall polished doors into a plush salon.

It had all happened so fast and the environment was so

different, compared to anything I was accustomed to, that it took me a few moments to absorb the fact that I was now inside the presidential palace, unescorted and about to meet a man whom I had last seen climbing into an airliner two and a half thousand miles away and almost ten years before.

President Mobutu Sese Seko, as he was now known, was standing talking to a young girl as I entered. He wore a smart grey safari suit this time, topped with the leopard skin hat that had become his trademark. The proud General I had met all those years before now had about him a new aura of power and looked every inch the suave President. He turned and came towards me, one hand outstretched in greeting, the other holding the hand of the girl whom he introduced to me as his daughter. He called her Minna.

His greeting was friendly and after a few moments he suggested we withdraw to his private apartment, deeper in the palace, where his wife was also waiting to greet me. With his daughter skipping beside him, he led the way, pausing briefly to exchange a few words with an aide who was waiting by the door. A few moments later we were in his private apartment. This, while still spacious, was quite spartan compared to the state rooms. There was furniture, of course, but it was relatively plain and had obviously been in use for more than a few years. The place also had that lived in feel, with odd domestic items lying about; a pile of children's toys in the corner of one room, a child's sock lying on a sofa and a partly completed jigsaw puzzle spread out on a table.

As we came into the private apartment two other children attached themselves to our little party and started chattering to their father. They, of course, were speaking in their local language, so I understood none of what they said, but their relaxed manner and his loving response was clear and natural. Mobutu led his little entourage through to a small courtyard garden, bright with bougainvillea and hibiscus, where two smaller children were teasing a fat white cat with a red flower, tied to a piece of string. Their mother was sitting on a stool watching them.

Madame Mobutu's command of French had improved considerably since the last time we had met in Nigeria. Then, she had only enough for the basic courtesies and "yes" or "no" mealtime responses. Now she spoke fluently as she came forward to take both my hands, her manner bright, open and smiling. She was dressed simply in a green dress, wore no jewellery, with a pair of cheap green rubber flip-flops on her feet. Although she had borne six children, she was still a slim woman, but had about her a certain style that needed no embellishment to show off her elegance. She was also relaxed, assured and in no way dominated by her husband, whose public reputation was one of tough authoritarianism and commanding charisma.

Marie Antoinette Mobutu was much loved in Zaïre and was popularly known as Mama Mobutu. Mobutu himself idolised her, although it was widely known that he had a number of mistresses, the chief among whom, Bobi Ladawa, became his second wife a few years later after the sudden and untimely death of Marie Antoinette from cancer at the age of forty-seven. Bobi Ladawa was also part of the household and I met her later that evening. The two women appeared to be good friends and easy in one another's company as well as with Mobutu and his children. Bobi Ladawa had already borne him several children by this time.

In years to come, Mobutu's reputation would deteriorate dramatically until he was clearly the tyrannical despot for which the world will undoubtedly remember him. By that time, Mama

Mobutu's public appearances would have diminished to almost zero. At this stage, however, she was still seen frequently at his side whenever he was out on public business, and he was still the national hero.

Madame Mobutu's attention wandered slightly and she smiled as her eyes bypassed me. I turned to see what had attracted her attention and saw the President sitting on the floor with three very small children climbing all over him as he tried to tickle them. They had pulled off his hat and one of his shoes, but he seemed quite unconcerned and appeared to be enjoying the game as much as the squealing children were.

I looked back at his wife, who merely shrugged and said, "Don't believe everything the foreign press prints about him. He may be tough when he is being a President, but in here he is a father like any other man. He makes time to play with them every day." She was clearly very fond and proud of him.

A few minutes later, one of the other female members of the household appeared in the doorway ringing a small bell. The game stopped immediately, each of the children embraced their father and they scampered away laughing. The President retrieved his lost shoe and dropped his hat on a chair, then led me further into the garden to where some chairs were set out under a wide canopied royal poinciana tree. Waving me to a seat, he dropped into a chair and called something over his shoulder. A few moments later his wife reappeared with a tray of drinks, which she placed on a small table.

"What will you drink?" she asked me.

I chose a local beer. The President chose a milky concoction that turned out to be a mixture of palm wine and pastis and his wife opened another bottle of beer for herself. It is unusual in most of Africa for the female members of the family to join in like this but, as I was to discover, this was an exceptional family in so many ways. In her home environment, Marie Antoinette Mobutu was the queen.

Sitting there in the President's garden felt slightly unreal, but it was not uncomfortable. He was the same affable man I had met previously and when, as now, he stepped out of his presidential role and into that of a family man, he was excellent and easy company.

He was already aware of the development projects that had brought me to Zaïre and he wanted to know more. For almost an hour he asked searching questions, listening carefully to my answers. In between these, he told me things about the country that he thought I should understand and described how he was trying to steer the population of some fifty-eight million people away from the abrasive tribalism that had been their lot since before the Belgians came and towards a new, home-grown nationalism with a unique and internally generated identity.

"Today," he explained, "if you ask any man who he is, he will say 'I am baLuba or I am baShongo or baPende' or whatever tribe he comes from. I want them all to say 'I am Zaïrois' and to be proud of belonging to this nation."

"Can they not do both?" I asked. "I am British, but I am also a Scotsman."

He smiled wryly. "And the Scots have tribes, I know, but you do not take the distinctions as seriously as Africans do. You should know that, you grew up with it."

It surprised me that he remembered this detail, but I remembered having to explain to him about my childhood and early years in East Africa, back in 1963 when he had insisted on interviewing me before accepting my services as interpreter, despite my father's assurances that I could do the job. The realisation that he had such a detailed and long memory made me view him in a new light. He may not have had much formal education, but he had an exceptional intellect.

"If the tribal conflict in our last civil war, before I became President, had not been so fierce, perhaps what you suggest may have been possible," he continued, "but these are people with strong passions and deep-rooted taboos. It is not easy to abandon these ways for something new."

That was why, he explained, agents of the *Mouvement Populaire de la Révolution* (MPR), Zaïre's only permitted political party, worked in every administrative sector to instruct the '*citoyens*' in their civic responsibilities. I was to find that 'citizen' was to become a very familiar form of address in this country.

"The agents of the MPR are there for people to go to with their problems," said the President. "In some isolated areas, they also have to administer the justice system and resolve disputes. You will see this in action when you get out into the country."

"I have heard that there are travel restrictions in some areas, Mr President," I began, "I'm sure your officials will have considered the logistics, but I hope the restrictions will not impede the work I am here to do. Do they apply in all areas?

"Not at all," the President replied smoothly. "We have a visa system in operation in the Kasai region, but this is only because that is the diamond mining area and it is necessary to have some controls to stop smuggling. But you will have no problems."

"I'm sure I won't," I lied. "Everyone has been very helpful since I arrived." I remembered the paranoia at the airport and the way his Tontons had come looking for me in my hotel. This was no liberal democratic state, and I suspected his description of how the MPR operated in the provinces was rather generous. I felt quite certain that control and indoctrination by the Party were the rule here rather than the motherhood and comfort he had implied.

He was a superb actor; I'll give him that. Anyone coming to Africa for the first time and receiving the sort of welcome I had had here might have been fooled into believing in Mobutu's dream. Anyone with just a little exposure to Africa would have realised that tribalism doesn't disappear so easily and, all too frequently, only tyrannical dictatorship can hold the different factions from one another's throats. Internecine squabbling, usually with machetes, spears and poisoned arrows, is a cultural imperative all across this continent. It was only marginally suppressed by colonialism and was now in the ascendant again as a means of settling disputes, achieving dominance and settling old issues demanding vengeance.

He reclaimed my attention by telling me about some of his grand development plans: a series of dams on major rivers to create huge lakes where fisheries projects would breed enough fresh fish to provide everyone with a reliable source of protein as well as hydro-electricity; major beef and dairy ranching schemes on the upland pastures to make proper use of the vast areas of grassland scrub where forest had been cut down; vast forestry schemes to plant noble hardwood trees to replace those taken by loggers; and huge plantations of oil palms to provide both food products and soap that would bring hygiene to the villages, reducing the burden on an inadequate health service.

"But Mr President," I interrupted him, "wouldn't it be better to start with clean water supplies for all the villages? It is difficult for people to be hygienic without clean water. This country is not short of water, it just needs cleaning but that requires a bit of work and some training. Soap has to be paid for and I wonder if the economy of the rural villages can support that. Most of them will already produce their own simple cleansing products anyway."

"That is the whole point," he smiled, looking at me as if I were a fly that had just walked into his spider's web. "By getting people to make proper soap and then buy and sell it, we not only develop a valuable industry, but it gets people actively participating in the country's economy. This generates commitment and a sense of shared purpose. We need that to build a strong national identity."

He was getting into lecturing mode now. "I want Zaïre to lead the way in Africa, and for our people to be proud of being Zaïrois. Later on we will use the dams on our rivers to make electricity for everyone. There is enough power in our rivers to make electricity for the whole of Africa, but first I have to break the inertia."

This, then, was part of his vision of ultimate power and I realised that his idea of thinking big was indeed to think on a global scale. Before, when I had met him in Nigeria, he had been a soldier and a competent General. Then, after a savage civil war, he had taken power and become President. He had at least brought some measure of stability to this most diverse and volatile of countries the size of western Europe, but at the price of an autocratic regime that was hardly based on democracy, however colourful the 'electioneering' that took place at regular intervals. Now, however, it was clear that he had much bigger ambitions and, if other African rulers were anything to go by, he was destined to become quite a tyrant. For a moment I wondered if his ultimate ambitions spread beyond his present borders.

This brief glimpse of the nascent despot was completely contradictory to the gentle family man who had invited me into his home and let me see him playing with his children like any other loving father. My reverie was interrupted by his wife announcing that food would shortly be ready. She insisted that I should stay and share the meal with the family; after all, she and her husband had been guests in my family's home the last time we had met.

The President led me to the dining area, a slightly untidy room. Its furniture bore the scars of family life; toys lay beneath the table. The cutlery was an assortment of cheap items that might have been bought in any African market, and the food was served in colourful enamel bowls that were certainly market bought.

A large new refrigerator stood in the corner and, as I took my place at the table, Mobutu opened this, selected two bottles of beer which he opened and then passed one to me. To each of the three teenage children who were already seated he passed an orange Fanta before pouring a glass of wine for his wife and taking his place at the head of the table. As he sat down, Bobi Ladawa joined us and took the empty place on his left. He introduced her but didn't explain her position in the household. Clearly some of the children round the table were hers.

Madame Mobutu passed around small enamel bowls containing a stew. This was apparently made of fish and chicken, which to me seemed a curious mixture.

"Is this your own recipe?" I asked.

"Not at all," she told me. "This is *gula mba'a*, which is a traditional dish from my home part of Zaïre in the north-west. It must contain fish and fowl, although the types vary, and we eat it with manioc *foufou* or mashed sweet potato. You can eat it with your hands, as many of our people do, or with a spoon if you prefer." I noticed that all the children were eating with spoons, while her husband was using his fingers.

When large bowls of *foufou* and sweet potato were passed to me, I helped myself to some of each and passed them on. Taking my cue from the President, I took a dollop of *foufou* with my fingers, rolled it into a ball, pressed my thumb into it to make a depression and scooped up some of the stew before putting it in my mouth. As a way of eating, this was nothing new to me, for I had been doing it since I was three and a half, when I first came to Africa. It did, however seem a little incongruous to be eating this way at the President's table.

Over supper the President asked me how I intended to approach my work in the interior. Although admitting that he had spent little time in Bandundu province, he seemed well informed about the region where I would be based and promised to give me a letter of introduction to the local Party agent. This man, he assured me, was energetic, well-liked and very effective at his job He was also local to the area and would certainly be a good man to have as my friend, and so he turned out to be. His name was Nkwanu Knaii.

He also talked about some of the cultural habits of the people among whom I was to work, which he evidently found quaint and not altogether appropriate for the people of a modern nation. His own people lived in an upland area a long way north, where the country was less densely forested and agriculture was more sophisticated. It was clear that he considered them superior in every way to the more primitive, forest dwellers of other regions. This was confirmed by the fact that he had insisted that his own language, Lingala, be adopted as the national language. He told me proudly that teaching it was now compulsory in every school throughout the country and it was rapidly replacing French as the official language of administration and government. To him, it made sense to have one of their own languages as the national language instead of the language of the former colonists. Zaïre was an independent African nation now and should be proud of its own national identity.

It was another of his initiatives to support his dream of uniting the population with one national identity. This had many facets and he explained that a return to traditional nomenclature was another element. As part of his doctrine of 'Africanisation' and 'authenticity', every citizen was required to abandon any foreign names they had previously used and take traditional African names. For this reason he had abandoned the Christian names, Joseph-Désiré, that he had been given at birth and he adopted the name Mobutu Sese Seko. His full name had Nkuku Ngbendu Wa Za Banga tacked on the end, but this was a bit of a gimmick, designed to promote the cult of Mobutu in the eyes of his people as a conquering hero. His wife was known as Mama Mobutu in public, but I noticed that he still called her Marie-Antoinette in private. She called him *"Mon Joseph"* or *"Mon mari"*.

It occurred to me that there were some similarities between Mobutu's doctrine of *'authenticité'* and something I had encountered before, Leopold Senghor's concept of 'Negritude'. This promoted the value of African identity as an equal to anything Western or Hamitic and maintained that Africans had an equal part to play in the future of the world where, since colonial times, they had been viewed as second-class subjects and before that were largely unknown to the rest of the world. Mobutu had lifted some of Senghor's ideas and moulded them to fit his own style, context and purpose and added a few more of his own invention. From all I had read about this country's history, I had found little to justify or provide historical basis for what he was now telling me.

Much of Africa adopted Christianity with some fervour during the colonial era. While in many places this adoption was only superficial and the people reverted to their animist, tribal beliefs as soon as the missionaries' backs were turned, in other areas the conversion was real and deeply entrenched. In those places, it provided something of a super deity and unified all the tribal and environmental spirits which so often found themselves in conflict. Along with this, a large number of new, quasi-Christian sects had grown up featuring indigenous prophets, saints and angels, yet copying the Christian tale and morality very closely for much of their doctrine. One of these, the Kimbanguist Church, was native to Zaïre and had many thousands of followers. I asked the President if this was to be promoted in his nation's cultural evolution.

"Religion is not the business of the state," he told me, "unless it seeks to meddle in government affairs. I, and my family, are Christians. The Kimbanguists also are Christians, but they have an extra prophet, who lived in this country back in 1926 and did some very holy, even miraculous, things. It is like the difference between Catholic and Protestant, except that it is African. The Kimbanguists run good schools and have a large farm school. You should visit them and see it. And they also respect the traditional beliefs of those people who are not converted. They are good Zaïrois; I let them be."

This sounded just a little too benign to me, and I wondered how he would behave if one of these sects appeared on the fringes of the political arena. It was all very well being tolerant, but any organisation that can command mass loyalty, combined with religious fervour, must surely come to be considered a threat by an autocrat. But he wasn't finished yet.

The President's face appeared everywhere, reinforcing what was in many ways a cult system.

"Some of our officials are members of this church," he continued. "They bring their comrades to the Party rallies and their leaders have also offered blessings for all those who attended. You see, they support our nation. They're not like the Muslims. We have very few of those in Zaïre and they are not liked because they view everyone else as inferior. Their doctrine will never take root here. We have some very good witch-doctors who will see to that!" He chuckled like a naughty schoolboy at this idea.

I wondered how he viewed the Protestant missionaries who had established more than forty missions in the country and ran several excellent bush hospitals. He did not seem inclined to discuss these and I had to accept that since he let them stay, they were viewed as benign and no threat to his rule.

Much later, when I had been in the country for almost a year, I discovered that he had several spies planted among the staff of every mission in the country. These were loyal members of the MPR, who reported everything that happened or was said, to their superiors in the Party's sector offices. These spies were often ignorant of each other's identities and so reported on each other as well as on the foreign missionaries.

Such insidious paranoia is typical of despots. I knew he would be taking an interest in my activities, but since the local MPR sector chief had by then become a good friend, I knew the President had an open access channel to find out about anything I did. Since I always kept my nose out of politics, I considered I had nothing to fear from this. This might sound naïve, because tyrants can be unpredictable, but *tant pis*: I could as easily be bitten by a poisonous snake in the jungle tomorrow. There was no point in worrying about what I couldn't control.

AFTER THE MEAL WAS FINISHED we adjourned to a seating area where Mobutu told me he liked to sit in the evening, to enjoy being with his children for a few minutes before they went to bed. Then he had to turn his attention back to official matters.

"There is too little time," he explained. "My officials keep intruding and requiring me to decide things for them."

And what would happen if they decided these things for themselves, I wondered. They would probably be in prison within minutes of his finding out. I realised that my impression of this man had changed greatly since the days when I had first met him. It had changed significantly this very evening, if truth were told. I had come here with memories of a charming and competent soldier whose command of authority was clear but not overbearing. Now he had revealed to me a man who had transformed himself from soldier into a politician with an agile mind and wide, all-embracing interests and an iron grip on everything that went on in his country. He might play at being the family man when it suited him, but I felt that this was now more of a fondly held memory than an everyday part of the man who was my host.

He interrupted my thoughts and I hoped that they had been sufficiently well-concealed not to give him reason to doubt me. His smallest children had been clamouring for his attention and he seemed to be absorbed in them.

"I enjoyed the time I spent with your father in Nigeria," he said, suddenly breaking off from the children and motioning for them to leave. They all went without argument, the older ones taking the smallest by the hand and dragging them out as they looked back, wishing they could stay.

"You also helped our discussions and made the visit profitable. Now I shall give you something that may be helpful for your work in my country. Sometimes the people who administer things can be a little over-zealous and make more difficulty than is necessary. I shall give you a letter that will resolve such difficulties, but ask that you only use it when there is no other solution. I do not do this very often, but I believe you are an honest man and will not abuse it." So saying he reached for a small bell that summoned a secretary.

The secretary who came was the young man who had met me at the door when I arrived. Mobutu gave him a stream of instructions in rapid Lingala and then asked me if I was carrying my passport. I handed it to him and he passed it on to the secretary.

"It is just so he can get the details right," he explained as the secretary left to do whatever he had been instructed. "Now, you must come back in daylight before you go into the forest. I have a fine garden here and also some animals you may like to see. The forest people gave me an *okapi* last year. It is a strange beast that hides all the time. There are also fine flowers and trees here."

"Yes sir," I said, "I saw a very fine salmon coloured bougainvillea as I came in. My mother would have liked one like that in her garden, which you may remember had many flowers."

"Then take a piece and send it to her," he laughed. "Now come. We will see if Nkukme has typed your letter."

He stood up and led the way out of the private apartment, back into the formal part of the palace, replacing his leopard skin hat as we went. His wife was nowhere to be seen now, so I was unable to thank her for her hospitality, but I thanked Mobutu and asked him to tell his wife how much I had enjoyed the meal. I wrote her a note later, when I was back in my hotel.

The secretary had finished typing the letter; I was surprised to see that it was in French. There was another copy of the same document underneath in Lingala. Mobutu signed both. He then took a large stamp from a locked drawer and applied it to each copy. He told me to give my mother's address to Nkukme who typed it on a large envelope to which the stamp was also applied.

"That envelope will let you send a piece of my bougainvillea to your mother without the post being held up," the President said, handing it to me together with his letter. "Please take a piece from the one by the door."

He shook my hand, said good night and was gone in an instant. The secretary was left to see me out to where the car that had brought me was waiting to take me back to my hotel.

Before climbing into the car I walked over and pulled off a generous piece of the bougainvillea. The Tontons looked slightly shocked at this liberty, but Nkukme told them I was doing it on the President's instruction and they backed down, looking at me speculatively as I climbed into their car. He must have said something else as well, for when we reached the hotel, they escorted me inside and one gave me a small card with a telephone number on it.

"If you encounter any problems while you are in Kinshasa," he told me, "ring this number. We will sort things out."

I must have looked slightly puzzled by this offer, so he added: "You are our President's friend."

With that both men saluted smartly and were gone.

8 ~ Jailbreak

IT ALL STARTED THE DAY I was passing the local police station at sunset and failed to notice that the national flag was being lowered. I didn't know it at the time, but everyone was required to stop what they were doing and face the flag for the two minutes the ceremony took. Failure to comply would result in immediate arrest if one was observed by a policeman, and this is exactly what happened to me at the beginning of February.

A policeman stepped out into the road in front of me and signalled for me to stop. Short of running him over, I had no choice, so I pulled up and waited for him to come around to the driver's side and explain what he wanted. He didn't. Instead, he came to the passenger side, opened the door and climbed in. With a broad smile, he instructed be to drive to the police station. Since he had spoken in Kituba, I played dumb and greeted him in French, for something told me he was probably just exploiting me to get a lift home.

By his gestures it was clear that he wanted me to start driving, so I put the Land Rover in gear and started forwards. That was the wrong direction. The excited policeman waved his arms

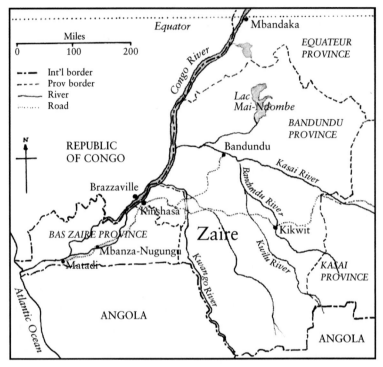

Western Zaïre showing major tributaries of the Congo River.

about, indicating that I should turn round and go the other way. With rapid and excited chatter and a lot of gesturing and pointing, he managed to direct me as far as the police station where he made me stop in front of the entrance. He piled out and demanded that I do the same.

Once more I pretended not to understand him, but he rushed around to the driver's door, pulled it open and took hold of my arm. He pointed inside the police station, yelling "*Tuer le moteur! Venez avec moi.*" I killed the engine, as he asked, and climbed out, locking the vehicle behind me and pocketing the key. Actually I dropped it down inside my waistband, ensuring that it slid into my underpants, in case they asked me to empty my pockets.

We went inside and he pointed to a bench and indicated that I should sit and wait. I sat, together with half a dozen other people, all of whom looked bored and had probably been there for hours. This, I thought, could turn out to be a long wait. I wondered what time these chaps go home.

It was almost an hour before the same policeman returned from the bowels of the building, pointed at me and gestured for me to follow him. I stood up slowly and he led me along a corridor, around several corners, to another waiting area to another bench occupied by three more bored-looking men. One was a man I had met before, in the bank, so naturally I said hello to him and asked what he was doing there.

"*Silence!*" bellowed a voice in French, before the man could reply. It came from inside an adjoining office, the door of which stood open. I ignored this and continued talking to my friend, for he had instantly assumed that status by sharing this predicament with me. This, however, was not what the person inside the office either intended or expected. He appeared in the doorway, looking cross and slightly menacing.

"*Vous parlez pas!*" he said emphatically.

"Why?" I asked in French. "Why have I been brought here?"

"Wait here," the man said. "And no talking. Anybody!" With this he disappeared back into the office.

This all seemed rather pointless and I had no idea why they had brought me here, so I got up and followed him in.

"Excuse me," I began, before anyone could say anything, "but could you please tell me why I have been brought in here and why you want me to wait. I have business to attend to and am expected at a meeting. I brought your policeman back, as he requested, but now, if you don't mind, I must go."

The three men in the office stared at me in silence for a few moments before the officer seated behind the desk addressed me. "You have committed an offence. That is why you are here. You will stay until I have investigated it."

"What offence?" I asked, still unaware of the importance of the flag business. "I was driving along, very carefully, when your officer jumped out into the road and made me stop. Then he insisted that I drive him here, which I did. What is this offence you now accuse me of? Helping get a lazy policeman back to the station?" I regretted this even before the words had left my mouth, for the man was standing there and, if he understood my French, he could, quite reasonably, get upset at my describing him as lazy.

"Let me see your driving permit," the officer behind the desk said, ignoring my questions until I took the required document from my pocket and put it on his desk. He examined it carefully and compared the photograph with me. Evidently satisfied that it was mine and that it was legal, he leaned back in his chair and looked at me.

"You failed to stop while the national flag was being lowered at six o'clock," he said. "That is why you are here."

I was amazed. "I didn't know the flag was being lowered and I couldn't even see any flag where I was," I protested. "And nobody ever told me I had to stop if someone is pulling it down."

"That is no excuse," the officer told me. "In this country everyone has to stop what they are doing and face the flag when it is being lowered in the evening. That includes foreigners."

"Well, thank you for explaining," I said, as politely as I could manage. "I am sorry I did not know this before, but in future I shall remember and make sure that I stop."

"And face the flag," the officer repeated. "Now wait outside."

"What for?" I asked, naively thinking that the business should now be over as the misunderstanding had been cleared up and I had apologised.

"Wait outside," the officer insisted, waving me out of his office.

I went out into the corridor, thought about it for a moment, then retraced my steps to the front entrance and went outside. Reaching inside my clothing, I retrieved my keys, unlocked the Land Rover and sat in the driving seat. After ten minutes nobody had come looking for me, but I had seen several policemen leave the building, one of whom looked very like the man who had leapt out and stopped me earlier. I waited another five minutes, then started the engine and drove home.

At this time I was living in a house that I rented from an old Portuguese trader. It was far larger than I needed, but its location on the edge of Kikwit was convenient, being next to the road leading down into the forest to the east of the town. This was where most of my work was located. I had eleven projects to provide clean drinking in outlying villages. While most of these were near rivers – everywhere was close to a river in this part of Africa's biggest rain forest – many of them had no consistently clean source of drinking water. As a result, waterborne diseases and infections were very common. My work was principally to teach people how to build simple but effective filters on their springs or to install filters in river beds that would enable people with pumps to draw clean water and help the public health outreach initiatives that were supposed to be running in the region.

I would have preferred to live in the forest villages where I worked, but for the moment had to put up with living in the town and wasting hours each day driving into inaccessible parts of the forest to work. To help with this, the government had provided me with a driver as well as a Land Rover. Unfortunately the driver, Téokuno Filéu, was not a local man, having been shipped in from one of the northern provinces. Although he was a pleasant fellow, he didn't know the roads and he didn't know the local language. I concluded that he was a minder rather than a useful member of the project and just resigned myself to having him about.

When he first arrived, I asked him about his name and he told me that he had made it up himself when President Mobutu had ordered everyone to abandon all European Christian names in favour of African names. The driver's name had been Théophile Vilanne, but he Africanised it to Téokuno Filéu. He was a good mission-educated lad and sounded as though he didn't much like this policy, so I decided just to call him Téo and he agreed with a huge grin.

I had left Téo in town that particular afternoon, for a lesson with the retired teacher who was teaching us both the basics of the local language. I was on my way to pick him up when the policeman had stopped me. He was curious to know why I was so late but philosophical when I told him.

"They just want to play with you, because you are a *mundele*," he said. "The old colons shout a lot when the police mess them about so they do it some more, just for fun. It happens everywhere."

"Do you think they will come looking for me, for just driving off?" I asked.

"They will have forgotten you by now," he said, "Until they see you again. Then they will stop you to ask why you didn't wait. It is only a game. If you object, they win." Téo thought the whole thing was a big joke.

He drove me home and then went off to wherever he had

found lodgings. The house I had rented was big enough for him to have used one of the rooms there, but he preferred to stay elsewhere. I assumed he had found himself some female companionship and preferred to keep it private. Unless, I thought, he really was my minder and was obliged to go somewhere and report on my day's activities and this gave him the perfect excuse to leave me and do this. Never mind, there was seldom anything really private in Africa, particularly in a dictatorship like Zaïre. Being a friend of the President did not exclude me from being watched, even if he and I did keep our acquaintance private. In fact, if anybody knew about it, this would be even greater cause for me to be watched, for I had been here long enough by now to realise that Mobutu Sese Seko was more feared than loved by his people. Anybody directly associated with him would therefore be treated with some measure of reserve, if not outright suspicion by everyone except those wanting to ingratiate themselves.

This was a comforting thought since, quite clearly, the local police had messed me around the way they would any other European. Everyone else with whom I dealt on a daily basis was quite open and friendly and most were keen for some involvement. Since I never discussed the President with anyone, nobody could have reason to think I knew more than his name.

THE NEXT MORNING I HAD to go through the town to a research station that was situated on the other side. On the way through, I stopped in the main street to visit one of the shops. When I came back to my vehicle there was a policeman standing beside it.

"You are violating the parking restrictions," he announced.

"What parking restrictions?" I asked.

He pointed to a circular notice along the street. "That notice is a parking restriction," he said. "You will come with me to the police station and pay the fine."

"What fine?"

"Five zaïres," he said, "for parking illegally. Now, we go." He indicated the Land Rover and it was clear that he expected me to drive him. I was tempted to say we should walk, but that might be pushing my luck too far when I still didn't know the rules of this game. Looking up and down the street, I could see there were about twenty other vehicles parked, on both sides of the road. The sign to which the policeman had pointed was one I had not seen before, being circular with one half painted white and the other dark blue. On the white half was a figure 1 and on the blue half a 2 was painted. I would have to get a copy of the local highway code, if such a thing existed, and look this up. With resignation, I drove him to the police station.

We went through a similar performance as the previous evening, with me sitting on a bench with a lot of other men who looked bored, talking and being told to be silent. After about half an hour, during which nothing happened, I just got up and left. Nobody seemed to notice my departure, and in my rear view mirror I did not see anyone come running out to stop me driving off, so I made my visit to the Chinese agricultural research station and then went to see my language teacher for two hours.

For the following two days I was down in the forest, leaving before dawn and back home late. Téo, who hated the forest, drove most of the way, but managed several times to take wrong turnings and get us very lost on indescribable roads. At least he said they were roads, but I thought he was following small stream beds. We did eventually manage to find three of the five villages we had set out to visit and received a warm welcome in each one. I noticed that each time the village elders invited me to walk further into the forest with them in order to inspect a water source, Téo found reason to remain in the village. He wasn't going to tramp around in the jungle for anything; it was full of creepy crawlies, snakes, nasty biting insects and plants that could attack you with thorns.

ON ONE PARTICULAR ROAD in Kikwit, there was a pair of traffic lights. They were old and tatty, with peeling paint and weedy creepers trying to climb their posts. The lights had not worked for years. In fact, one of the old traders who had lived in the town for more than forty years, told me that they had never worked. Never mind, to the inventive African mind, this was another potential source of amusement, as I found out a few days later. I was driving along that road, on my way to the bank, and had just passed the traffic lights when a policeman stepped out into the road and flagged me down.

I stopped and he came to the window beside me.

"Traffic infraction," he announced, before I could even say hello.

"What infraction?"

"You failed to stop for the traffic lights," he said, with a straight face.

"But they don't work! Nobody ever stops there!"

"It is still an infraction; you failed to stop," he insisted. "Take me to the police station and you can pay the fine there." As he said this, two other cars passed us and he made no attempt to stop either.

"What about those cars? They failed to stop. Why don't you

arrest them?" I protested lamely, realising as I did so that it was pointless. He was, as Téo had predicted, playing the game. I opened the passenger door for him and we drove to the police station and I was already seating myself on the bench inside the door before he told me to sit and wait.

Looking around the other people waiting on those benches, I recognised a couple of faces. Their owners had been there the last time I was arrested. I smiled and nodded to them and received shy grins of recognition in return. None of them spoke and when I asked the man next to me if he had been there long, a voice from an adjoining office with its door open called for silence.

After ten minutes I got up and quietly left. My Land Rover was parked about thirty metres along from the door and nobody came after me before I reached it, so I didn't even bother looking back this time.

When I got back to the house, Téo told me that I was required to report to the local office of the MPR to be interviewed by the Chef de Secteur. This was the local political commissar. I had registered in the locality with him when I arrived, as foreigners were required to do, which left me wondering now why I was being summoned. Was this a new facet of the game?

Téo drove me to the MPR office, which was situated in a scruffy building on a quiet side street with an untarred surface. About half the streets in town had tarred surfaces, but there seemed neither rhyme nor reason about how they had been chosen. The main street was surfaced for only half its length, and that was not where the older, more prominent buildings were. Although there was plenty of space in front of the building, Téo stopped some distance away and said he would wait there until I came out. When I asked him why he didn't just stop outside the door, he spat out of the window. "They are even more corrupt than the police, those people. I want nothing to do with them."

"But you are a member of the MPR," I said, "I have seen your card."

"Everybody is a member; that is obligatory," he sounded resentful, "But I don't have to like it or to believe what they preach."

This was a new side of Téo that I had not seen before. I wondered if I had been deluding myself about him being my minder, but this was not the moment to explore that. I was expected in the office along the street and a man sitting by the door had seen us pull up. The people inside would certainly know I was coming and wonder if I delayed.

My summons to the MPR office turned out to be nothing sinister. It was simply that the *chef de secteur* wanted to meet me. He had been away when I had come to register and I had only met his assistant. Nkwanu Knaii was a couple of years older than me, had been educated in Belgium, and seemed friendly, open and progressive. He came from this region and was keen to support any development work being done to help his people, particularly those who lived in the deep forest. We had an easy hour's discussion and I left with him saying that he would like to accompany me, one day soon, to see for himself the work I was doing. Later on Nkwanu Knaii and his family became very good friends and his children adopted me as their white uncle.

When I got back to the Land Rover, Téo was sceptical. It seemed that he really didn't like any authority and had only taken the job as my driver because it was paid by the government and this status therefore offered him a certain amount of protection against some vague menace that was never really made clear.

Never mind, while I was learning my way he was a useful 'gofer' and good company. I had already thought of moving to live down in the forest and suspected that he would then return to the city. There were times when he was more of a fish out of water here than I was.

TWO DAYS LATER, TÉO got drunk in a seedy bar and became involved in an altercation that got him arrested and carted off to the local prison. I went down to see if I could bail him out. The warder told me that if I paid a fine of five zaïres and picked him out from the crowd inside, I could have him. He unlocked a huge door, which required the use of three large keys, and took me inside. There were about ninety prisoners milling about in a large yard and it took me a couple of minutes to find Téo. While I was looking for him, I noticed a pale figure huddled in a corner. He looked like a white man, but could equally have been an albino. I asked the warder who he was.

"Some *mundele* who has been here a couple of years or so," he said, not really interested.

"Does he have a name?" I asked.

"Don't know," the man was bored with my interest. Keeping people locked up was his job, who they were or why they were there didn't matter.

Before coming down to Kikwit from the capital, Kinshasa, I had heard a number of stories of people who had mysteriously disappeared in the interior. Some had been missing for six or seven years, others had vanished more recently. According to the scuttlebutt, none had ever reappeared and most were presumed dead. Could this man be one of these people?

Téo didn't know much more. He said the man was definitely a

mundele and spoke French with a strange accent. He might be Canadian. Téo had spoken to the man briefly, but did not know why he was there or what his name was. The other prisoners called him Piasanne.

The rumours I had heard told of a Canadian who had disappeared two and a half years previously, but I couldn't remember his name. I wondered if this could be the same man, but then remembered that he was supposed to have disappeared about eight hundred kilometres further east in a mining area. For the next two days, the thought kept niggling at the edge of my thoughts until finally I decided I would have to find out.

I went to the prison and asked the warder to speak to the man and ask, saying that the family of a colleague of mine who was missing were worried and I had been asked to enquire if this was the same man. The warden was not interested, but when I pulled a packet of American cigarettes from my pocket to offer him one, managing to drop a five zaïre note on his desk he told me to ask him myself, quickly pocketing the note as he steered me towards the door.

The man was still huddled in the same corner and looked slightly alarmed as we approached. He was indeed the missing Canadian and his name was Simon Piersen. He was a geologist from Quebec and had been working on a hydroelectric scheme near Lubumbashi when he had been snatched by armed men one night and dragged off to a jail. Since then he had been moved a couple of times, but could not say how long he had been here. He didn't even know where here was. I asked if he had family and he told me he had a wife back at home who was pregnant at the time he had been captured. I asked for details and he told me, but I didn't write anything down to avoid attracting undue attention.

The warden was standing by the door waiting for me and asked if it was my colleague.

"No," I said. "I can't make sense of that fellow. He seems to be slightly mad. You can keep him." I offered him another cigarette, neglecting to reclaim the packet when he accepted. I said goodbye and left the prison.

For the next few days I mulled over the problem. Meanwhile the police continued to harass me. The following week I had to make a flying visit to Kinshasa. Téo dropped me at the airport where I gave him instructions to stay sober and out of jail so he could meet the return flight in two days time.

In Kinshasa I made a few enquiries at the consulate, since it was responsible for all Commonwealth citizens in the country except for the Indians and Australians, who had their own representation. They knew of Simon Piersen, but told me that he had walked out on his job and gone home without telling anyone. They knew nothing else and had evidently not bothered to enquire. When I told them he was in prison in the interior, they flatly denied that this was possible and said I must be mistaken. I argued the case for a few minutes but got precisely nowhere. As far as the consulate staff were concerned, the man had gone home and that was the end of the matter. I don't think I was very popular by the time I left the consulate that day.

My meeting that afternoon was with the government hydrological service, who had promised to provide me with detailed maps of my working area, together with a lot of useful hydrological data. It was a relief to talk to people who were interested in their work after those standoffish diplomats, so I forgot about Simon Piersen for a few hours.

The next morning, I went to the central telephone office and put through a coded call to a contact in London who could find the answers to most questions, asking her to make enquiries and send a telegram to me in Kikwit, with suitably cryptic answers to my questions.

On the flight back to Kikwit I sat thinking about all the occasions when the local police had harassed me. I would never consider them universally corrupt, although it was evident that there was an element of this but, as I had discovered some weeks before when I had had something stolen and reported it, they could be more than diligent in seeking out and capturing the culprit. Their methods, although highly questionable, got results and I had no intention of being on the wrong side of such an investigation. At the same time, I realised that if they were playing with me, as they had for the last few weeks, they were probably reasonably disposed towards me. After all, it wouldn't do for either them or I to spoil the game, would it? So could I work the game to my advantage, spring the man quickly and be back in town doing something innocuous that would allow them to continue the game without suspicion? It was a hell of a risk, but if London gave me the green light, it might just be possible

Téo met my plane and handed me a telegram. I waited until we were outside before opening it. It read: 'MARIANNE AND ELISE BOTH WELL AND STILL LONGING FOR NEWS OF S. HOPE YOU CAN ASSIST. MARJORIE.'

To me this was as good as an instruction to get him out. The message confirmed what I had hoped and saved me from agonising over the decision. Simon Piersen had a wife and daughter waiting in Canada, just hoping, hoping, hoping that one day he would come home safely. The child had never seen her father and he didn't even know that he had a daughter. By the time we reached the house, I had decided that he would meet her; it was now simply a matter of how to make that happen.

TRYING TO SPRING FROM jail a man who the authorities and his own consular representatives denied even existed was not going to be a straightforward business. By all conventional means, it was probably not possible. In this country, where people could disappear without trace so easily, he was liable to vanish again the moment I made an approach for his release. In fact, the enquiry I had made a few days previously could have started that process already. I realised that time could be short. I needed help and the only person I could think of to provide it was Téo. His hostility to authority could be useful; I just hoped it was genuine.

I thought about it overnight and on and off all through the next day, while we were down in the forest. On the way home that evening, I broached the subject with Téo and asked for his help. It didn't take long for him to warm to the idea and he made a number of helpful suggestions. When he dropped me off at my house, I gave him some cash and he went into town to buy supplies. Meanwhile I told my neighbours that I was going off into the forest for a week and so would not be around. I asked them to keep an eye on the house and to let anyone who came looking for me know where I had gone. Then I went to my tool store behind the house to sort out some items that would be useful.

Téo returned and we packed my collection into the back of the Land Rover. On the back seat he had piled several cartons of cigarettes, three cases of tinned beer and a carton of sardines, together with several loaves of bread and some plastic bags with assorted items in them. Everything, he assured me, would be very well received when delivered to the prison yard. We drove to the other side of town and I dropped Téo off near the bar that had been the scene of his recent arrest. It was nearly nine o'clock when I dropped him; he reckoned it should take him less than three hours to get arrested again and be back in jail.

"What happens if they take you to the police station and not to the prison?" I asked, looking for things that could go wrong.

"The prison is nearer," he said. "Late at night they will be tired and lazy. They will take me to the prison and leave me until the morning or until you find out and come to get me. Like last time." His logic fitted everything I had so far learned about the police behaviour, so I left him and went home.

At midnight I let the Land Rover roll silently down the hill from my house and only started the engine at the bottom, then drove by a circuitous route round the outside of the town and stopped about a hundred metres from the prison, behind a dense clump of bushes. Taking all the supplies that Téo had stacked on the back seat and a rope from the back, I made my way round to the back wall of the prison, where I dropped the rope. The rest of the stuff I carried round to the side of the great rectangular enclosure and counted off the paces from the corner. I put down my burden, sat down and listened.

It was too dark to see my watch, but I reckoned it must have been about half past one when the singing started. It sounded like drunks on their way home on a Saturday night and was a most reassuring sound. Téo had achieved the first part of the plan. I waited a couple of minutes and then walked round to the entrance and asked to see the duty warden.

As it happened it was the same man I had met on my previous visit to release Téo. Once more I parted with a packet of cigarettes as I asked for the release of my drunken driver. I paid the fine, dropping an extra note on the floor as I extracted the one to pay the fine, just to hasten the process, and Téo was released. As we left the prison office and were let out of the gate, for the benefit of any warders who might be listening, I made a great show of telling Téo loudly that he was a useless drunk and that if he did this once more he would lose his job. The moment the heavy gate was closed behind us we ran for the corner and round to the side of the prison. Reaching the pile of things I had deposited earlier, we started throwing them over the wall. Cartons of cigarettes were followed by cans of beer, loaves, more beer, tins of sardines and the plastic bags. As fast as we could manage it we hurled everything over the four-metre wall.

With only a few items left to despatch, I left Téo to throw them and ran to the corner and along the back wall. There was, by now, a tremendous racket going on inside the prison yard as I picked up the coil of rope. I paused to make sure I had not got it caught on anything. Then I took a firm grip of one end and threw the rest over the wall. Téo joined me as I felt a strong tug on the other end of the rope. We both held on tight as somebody climbed the rope from the other side. Moments later a figure appeared on top of the wall and dropped to the ground. It was not, as I had expected, Simon the Canadian, but another man. He took hold of the rope and pushed me aside. Téo told me to let go and help Simon, who was now on top of the wall and seemed to be having problems. I learned later that while he had been inside the jail, Téo had arranged for this man to help with the rope.

Simon almost fell the last part of his descent. I caught him and ushered him away towards the Land Rover. As I unlocked it, Téo joined us and helped me get the Canadian into the back and cover him with a blanket and a roll of palm matting. He told me that a number of other men had come over the wall behind us and that this was turning into a mass breakout. It might distract attention from what we had done, but then again, it could be a lot more serious for us if the truth about what had happened ever came out. I just hoped the escapees would be ineffective at hiding themselves and the police would be as lazy as they appeared and not try too hard to investigate. We had probably left a trail of clues a blind man could see.

With me driving, we headed as quietly and sedately as the adrenalin would allow towards the eastbound road. We drove steadily for half an hour and then stopped to check on our passenger. He was dishevelled and dirty, very thirsty and also very confused. Téo rearranged things in the back compartment so that he could lie down and we put some padding down for him to lie on. With a few bits of wood braced across sideways we were able to leave him space to lie in comfort, but with a covering of the palm matting and a few baskets to disguise the fact that there was anything else in the back. I gave him a couple of water bottles and a packet of sandwiches I had made earlier, reassured him that he was free and that we were going to send him home, and then we drove on.

There were eleven ferries on the road we were taking from Kikwit to Kinshasa. Normally they were at the far side when you reached them, with several vehicles, usually overloaded trucks, waiting to cross. Amazingly, the first five ferries were not only on our side of the river, but there was nothing waiting, so we were able to cross without delay. In all we managed to get across seven ferries before dawn.

As it got light, we pulled off the road in an isolated spot to

Ferry lights: crossing the Kwango River on the road to Kinshasa.

check on our passenger. He had slept a bit, but was still desperately tired and once more in need of sustenance. Téo lit a small fire and we brewed coffee and made some porridge.

It occurred to me after Simon had greedily consumed a large bowl of porridge that we should have rationed him. He was obviously not used to having plenty of food and the volume alone might upset him. I suggested he should not eat the banana that Téo had given him, but it was too late, he had already started and wasn't going to stop. It was the first fruit he had eaten in over two years. The coffee was pure luxury to him and it was probably this, freely given, that finally convinced him that he was free. He wanted to ask questions, but I told him these would have to wait. If we were to get him home safely it must be done fast, and I was still not sure how later stages of the plan would pan out because I actually had no arrangements in place. There is an old African proverb that says 'Every bird must fly on its own wings', and that is just what I was doing now. If things went wrong, I had only one trump card, my letter from President Mobutu, and I was far from certain how effective that would be if I was caught helping an escaped prisoner. Perhaps I too would disappear.

We loaded Simon back into the Land Rover, gave him fresh water bottles, covered him up and were back on the road within forty-five minutes. Three hours later we arrived at the eighth ferry and there was a problem. We were at the back of a long line of trucks and a few smaller vehicles. At the front of the line was a convoy of military trucks and the road was full of soldiers.

I was driving at the time and, as I pulled up, Téo leapt out and went forward to talk to some of the soldiers. He came back a few minutes later to tell me the news and predict that we would be stuck there for a long time. The river was too low to allow any of the heavy trucks to cross as the ferry kept grounding on a sand bar. Nothing had gone across for several hours and the ferry was presently on the other side, waiting for the river to rise.

"Could it manage a small vehicle like ours?" I asked.

"Probably," Téo replied, "but all these trucks are in front of us and the army are in front of them. We will have to wait."

I wondered. Maybe this was the situation for which Mobutu had given me the letter I carried.

"I'll go and ask," I said. "Stay here and ask Simon to keep quiet. He'll have to remain under cover until we pass this lot." So saying, I climbed down and headed up the road towards the ferry.

Soldiers called out greetings to me as I passed their trucks and I replied, feeling more confident with the language now. I stopped and asked one Captain where they were headed. He said they were going to a base just this side of the capital. He didn't sound too enthusiastic about it either.

"Oh, do you mean General Bumba's headquarters?" I asked, brightly.

"Yes. What do you know of him?" the Captain asked.

This General was one I had heard of. He was the commander of the western brigade and reputedly a tough man to serve under. There had been trouble at one of his bases the previous year and his action in sorting it out had been ruthless. Perhaps the Captain had reason to be less than ecstatic about his posting.

"I am told he is a very good General," I told him. "In fact I am going to the same place. There has been a problem with the water on the base. I am a water engineer and the President himself has asked me to help," I continued, putting my neck on the line. "Do you think your commander would be able to help me get across the river soon? I'm sure you would like to find clean water when you arrive at the base."

The Captain looked slightly surprised as I pulled the letter from my pocket and held it so that he could see the presidential seal and the signature.

"I will ask the Colonel," he said swiftly, perhaps assuming that anyone with a letter bearing this seal and signature might be important. He strode off towards the head of the column and I followed a yard behind him.

It took us five minutes to find the Colonel and less than that time for him to decide to help me. He did ask several times that I should tell General Bumba how helpful he had been when I got there and I assured him that I would certainly do so. A soldier was sent running back to tell my driver to bring the vehicle to the front of the line and to make sure the way was clear.

I gave a cigarette to the Captain and the rest of the packet to the Colonel while complimenting him on how well he managed his column and how well-mannered his soldiers had been as I walked up the line. He was a happy man by the time Téo brought the Land Rover up and he sent a man down to the river to summon the ferry across. Since it was only to carry one light vehicle, he would accept no refusal from the ferryman. This worthy obviously got the message and moments later the ferry started towards us.

Making a slight show of writing down the names of both the Colonel and his Captain, I again promised to give a glowing report to General Bumba and we drove onto the ferry. My relief was enormous when we reached the far bank and Téo drove up the slope. With a quick wave to the Colonel, we resumed our dash for the capital.

Ten kilometres down the road we stopped in a patch of forest to relieve ourselves and then a few kilometres later bought some food from a roadside shop. With the minimum of delay and only a brief check on our passenger, we drove on, taking it in turns to drive and changing over at each ferry.

It was five o'clock when we passed the turning for the base where the army convoy was bound. Less than an hour later we reached the outskirts of Kinshasa and stopped at a Texaco station for petrol. By the time we got into the city, the consulate was closed and the embassy also. I decided that we had better go to the ambassador's residence. He could provide sanctuary for Simon Piersen and later arrange his onward travel home.

Arriving at the residence, we found the place lit up like a fairground and a pair of smart Royal Marines manning the gate. I showed my passport and asked to see the Ambassador on a matter of great urgency.

"I'm sorry, sir," replied the marine, "You won't be able to see him tonight. It's the Queen's birthday party and unless you have an official invitation, you can't come in. I don't suppose you have one, sir?"

"No, I've just arrived from the interior."

"Then perhaps you'd like to drop in to the embassy in the morning, sir," the marine was scrupulously polite.

"This won't wait till then. Perhaps you could just let me speak to the ambassador on your telephone." I said.

"I expect he's rather busy, sir," the man was adamant. "It's either the embassy in the morning or try the telephone from your hotel after ten-thirty tonight, but don't blame me if you get told where to go. His Excellency isn't likely to be too pleased at getting late night phone calls after his party."

"Could you just ring the house and ask for me, please?" I insisted. "This is extremely urgent and vitally important to British interests."

"Very well, sir," he was obviously having to work hard to keep his temper. "Just get your driver to pull over there so that other guests can get in, while I ring the residence." He pointed to a space to one side, outside the gate.

As Téo parked the Land Rover, the marine went into his gatehouse and picked up the phone. A couple of minutes later he was back saying the ambassador was not available. I asked him to try again and to get me at least one of the senior embassy staff on the line. Reluctantly he went to the phone again. After about five minutes he leaned out of the cabin and beckoned me over, holding out the receiver, stretched to the end of its wire. It was clear he wasn't going to let me inside the gate.

The voice on the phone turned out to be a disgruntled second secretary who listened to my story and then told me to bring Simon to the embassy in the morning.

"And what am I supposed to do with him until then?" I asked, the frustration creeping into my voice.

"You should have thought of that before springing him, shouldn't you, old boy," the voice said, loaded with sarcasm. Then the line clicked and went dead.

Typical British diplomats, I thought. Don't get involved and don't bother helping people with problems. This was not the first time I had come across this attitude. The gutless sods, I thought. Well, maybe someone else would help.

I KNEW THAT THE Australian representative was an ardent republican and hoped this would make him boycott the Queen's birthday party, always assuming that he got an invitation in the first place. I got back in the Land Rover and told Téo where to go. It took us a few minutes to find the right road, since many of the roads in the capital had no name boards, but twenty minutes later I was ringing the bell at the Australian consulate, with the Canadian and Téo beside me. There were lights in an upstairs room, so I kept my finger on the bell. After two minutes the window opened and an angry Australian voice demanded to know who I was and what I wanted.

"I have a distressed Canuck here who needs urgent help from a fellow Commonwealth member because the bloody Poms are too busy getting pissed for the Queen's birthday," I shouted back, doing my best to copy the Aussie accent.

"No worries there! Hold on, mate. I'll be right down," the voice had changed from hostility to one of genuine concern. The window closed and moments later other lights started coming on. In less than a minute the door opened and the three of us were ushered inside. The door closed behind us immediately and we were shown into a room a few paces down the hall.

The consul looked at us in turn. "Strewth, mate! You look a bit done over. Want a beer or d'ya need something else?" he asked, looking at Simon. I pushed a chair towards Simon and explained what had happened and how the present situation had come about, as briefly as I could. Téo waited quietly, not understanding the English.

"Right," said Bruce – the consul's name really was Bruce! – in a businesslike manner. "Let's get Simon to a bath and find some clean duds, then we'll sort out what to do about getting him home. It shouldn't be too difficult."

This was music to my ears. I like a man who starts from the premise that something is achievable and the only real question is 'How?' With a bit of luck, this crazy gamble would work out satisfactorily after all.

Bruce took Simon off into the bowels of the building and handed him over to his wife. He returned a few minutes later carrying three cans of beer, gave one each to Téo and me, then sat down to discuss plans.

"Have you eaten?" he asked.

"Not for about seven hours," I said.

"Right, food first then. Presumably Simon has no papers?"

"Correct."

"Right, I'll issue him some. He'll have to be an Aussie for a few days, but it'll see him home. I'll get on the wires in a minute and make some arrangements. Given what you've told me, I think we'd better get him out as fast as possible. It might be better to send him over the river and out through Brazzaville. That way his trail will go cold here." With this he left us to relax with our beer while he went through to his office to set things in motion.

Téo and I sat and dozed for half an hour until Bruce's wife, Sharma, came and called us to come up to their flat. She had cut Simon's hair and made him look respectable, found him some decent clothes and prepared a meal for all of us as well.

Bruce joined us a few minutes later. He told us he had made arrangements with a colleague in Brazzaville to receive Simon when he crossed the river and to send him onwards. He would be flown out to Australia and home from there. He had also arranged for someone to contact Simon's wife and let her know that he was safe and on his way home. With luck, confirmation of that should come through before he left here in an hour or so. He had prepared a load of papers to make everything look official and only needed to make a few more arrangements before Simon could be on his way.

This man is good, I thought. He doesn't hang about. I looked at Simon, but he seemed a bit bemused. I suppose being incarcerated and isolated for so long had cut him off so totally from the real world that he must have given up hope. In the last few hours, so much had happened that he was now confused and hardly daring to hope that what was happening was real.

These thoughts were interrupted by Bruce saying that he needed photographs in order to prepare a passport and other documents for Simon. They left the table together and Simon returned a few minutes later to finish his meal. He was desperately tired and his responses were slow. Sharma noticed this and brought him a pill.

"Get that down your neck, Simon. It'll wake you up and keep you going for another few hours, until Tony picks you up on the other side," she said. "Don't look so worried," she added. "I was a pharmacist before I married Bruce. It's only a pepper; I wouldn't give you anything dangerous, particularly not in your state. Tony'll get you checked over by a decent doctor before he sends you home, so you'll be all right." She was warm and reassuring and I noticed the relieved look in Simon's eyes as he accepted the pill and swallowed it.

Bruce came back again with a big grin on his face and a telex in his hand. He was enjoying all this.

"Well, the news is all good so far. I'm just waiting for one small cog to slip into gear and you can be off, mate," he told Simon. "Oh, I thought you'd like this. Your wife's coming to meet you in Oz." He handed him the telex.

Simon read it slowly, his finger tracing the words. I noticed tears in his eyes as he silently passed the telex to me. It was from his wife, written in French, and read: 'Have never lost hope. My joy will be complete when I meet you with our lovely Elise in Australia. Marianne.' I read it and passed it to Téo, who grunted and passed it to Sharma.

"That's nice," she said. "A reunion in Sydney; I think you all deserve that."

A bell rang somewhere else in the building and Bruce went off to answer it. He was back a few minutes later, bristling with enthusiasm.

"Ready to go home then, mate?" he asked Simon. "The transport's ready."

We all went downstairs, said our goodbyes to Sharma and climbed into the Land Rover. Bruce gave Téo directions and in about fifteen minutes we drew up in a quiet spot beside the river. A number of canoes and other boats had been hauled out on the bank and there was a large motorboat in the water with its engine ticking over.

Bruce approached the boatman and showed him a bundle of currency. There was a brief conversation, of which I understood nothing, and then Bruce handed the boatman a couple of notes, ripped the rest of the bundle in half and gave him one of the halves. The man accepted these and then indicated that his passenger should board. Bruce gave Simon a packet of papers, shook his hand and wished him luck. Simon came over to Téo and me and shook our hands.

"It sounds inadequate to just say thank you when you have done so much, but I don't know any other words," he said. "You are two crazy men and I thank God that you found me."

"Just send me a postcard to say you got home safely," I said. "Good luck." I pressed a card into his hand with my home address on it.

Téo embraced him. "Go and find your wife and child," he said and pushed him towards the boat.

The three of us watched, waving, until the boat was out of sight in the darkness before returning to the Land Rover and driving back to Bruce's flat.

"We should hear in about an hour and a half," he told us as we climbed the stairs. "I think we'd better have a beer while we wait."

I asked about the business with the banknotes. Bruce explained that he had promised the boatman that he would replace the torn halves with new notes when he returned with a receipt from the man who was waiting on the other side of the Congo River. He had used this technique before to ensure that something, or someone, reached the other shore in safety and it worked well. He should receive a telex in about an hour and a half confirming the delivery and then we would go back to the river. The boatman would return with a signed note from Tony saying that Simon had been delivered safely. Then Bruce would give him the rest of his five hundred zaïres.

"Not bad for a couple of hours work," I commented. "That must be about nine months' earnings."

"Cheap at twice the price," Bruce laughed. "Australia is honoured to help. Anyway, I'd gladly pay four times that, if it upset Her Majesty's pompous diplomatic poodles! Have another beer."

A few beers later, Bruce checked his telex and received the confirmation that Simon was safe. We returned to the river bank and paid the boatman and then went back to Bruce's flat to sleep for a couple of hours before starting on the long road to Kikwit. By the time we woke up, it was late afternoon so I told Téo we would go to a hotel for the night and leave early the next morning. Bruce wouldn't hear of this and insisted that we stay with him.

"You're okay for a Pom," he said, laughing. "You don't whinge and you get on and do what needs doing, and that counts in my book. Your mate's a good fella too," he nodded towards Téo.

When we passed the turning to the military base the following day, Téo turned to me with a mischievous look on his face.

"I hope the military convoy got through before now. Otherwise we will meet them and you will have some explaining to do to the Colonel."

Six months later, a note came from Canada. Its words were brief, but the message it brought was worth a ton of gold: "Thank you is inadequate, but we say it, every day. Marianne, Elise, Simon."

9 ~ Caravan to Taoudéni

NARROW RIBBONS OF SAND lie diagonally across the road going northwards out of Timbuktu, blown by the wind to fill the slight hollows of the undulating stony desert. There is little proper soil in this parched land although, in Roman times, the cultivated belt that once surrounded the ancient mud city was said to extend further than a man could ride his ass between sunrise and sunset. Cultivation, however, ceased here many hundreds of years ago when the mighty Niger River abandoned the city, changing its course to flow in a different channel which now lies fifteen kilometres to the south. What few trees grew here were soon cut down to provide fuel for cooking fires and the harsh desert wind scoured the thin topsoil, driving it southwards as pale dust to be lost over a million square miles of savannah, woodland and rain forest.

Now the land is stark and bare, with nothing but a few small rock outcrops and occasional low ridges to spoil the endless uniformity of the dull greyish terrain. Indistinct lines, where the small stones that litter the surface have been brushed aside by the shuffling feet of generations of camel trains, offer a modest

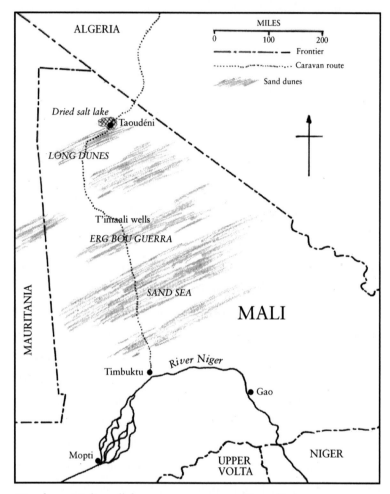

Northern Mali and the caravan route to Taoudéni.

indication of the trade route northwards. These divide and rejoin with random frequency so that from above it looks as if some giant net had been stretched out and laid on the ground like an enormous stencil.

The stones, where they lie, are mostly small with rounded edges and smooth surfaces, their roughness polished away after centuries of being rolled and jostled along the ground by the abrasive wind. Small wispy clumps of grass stand in isolated splendour where they have managed to survive the nibbling jaws of the countless grazing animals driven northwards to provide the traders with milk and meat as they travel with the trading caravans. Over the millennia the grasses have adapted, surviving now on the meagre ration of water they can absorb through their few leaves when insubstantial and infrequent mists humidify the desert air as it cools during the night. Like the landscape, these grasses too are grey. The thin scrub that once dotted this land, even within living recall, is now no more than a memory and the terrain stands empty.

There is another track northwards from Timbuktu that was supposed to be passable by motor vehicles, but few used it in the 1970s when I went there. Within the first day, we passed the skeletons of five abandoned cars and eleven wrecked lorries. Just why they broke down remained unknown and long forgotten. They stood as a stark warning to people who would travel this road that the desert is a mighty adversary and not something to be treated lightly. Technology is more likely than the traditional forms of transport to founder and fail, taking the lives of the travellers as well as their machines. Human bones in the front seat of one skeletal wreck sat in bleak testimony to the reality of this.

Looking ahead as I walk, I see an endless line of laden camels shuffling onwards; following, nose to tail, along whatever path was chosen by the one in the lead, possibly several miles ahead. They carry supplies of food and equipment that will be traded at the Taoudéni mines for huge blocks of salt. They also carry enough food for the return or onward journeys; there are no supplies where we are going and every traveller must go prepared.

Behind me, the caravan stretches out another mile or so, with women and children in the rear, driving small herds of fat-tailed sheep and skinny black goats which will provide the caravan with milk and meat during the journey out and back, although a few may be traded with the miners before the caravan returns.

The dull mud ramparts of the city are far behind us now, hidden by a low ridge that we passed soon after sunrise. We expect to cover about twenty miles a day and from this point on we will see no permanent habitations until we approach the great salt mines at Taoudéni, more than four hundred miles to the north. There are a number of watering points along our route, where we may meet other travellers who have paused and erected their black goat-wool tents, but otherwise we will have only each other, with the stars above us by night for cold company and the searing sun, glaring down on the desert by day.

Most of the camels are well-rehearsed in the caravan's routine and, even when not roped together, follow the one in front. This leaves the men who accompany them free to tramp in small groups, at times silent, at other moments alive with the vigorous discussions that seem to delight all desert dwellers. There is never any shortage of subjects for their discourses, which range from obscure points of philosophy or religion to the finer points of breeding camels and the mundane artistry of loading them correctly. Only in the hottest part of the day, or during the intermittent dust storms, does the level of conversation subside. Then each man travels alone with his thoughts, attending only to the laden beasts of which he is in charge.

WHEN WE LEFT TIMBUKTU, our caravan numbered close to five hundred camels, under the care of sixty-one men and boys who ranged in age from fourteen to eighty-one. The oldest, Alhadj Mehmet Alu, was the father of the caravan master. He had travelled this route twice a year for the last sixty-nine years and, while much of the terrain was familiar to him, he stoutly maintained that he had never followed exactly the same route twice. On only two occasions had he not made the trip twice in the same year, but in both these cases he had missed one salt caravan by leading another in an easterly direction on the Haj to Mecca.

Mehmet Alu was a scholarly man who could talk at length about a thousand subjects. His two favourite ones were his camels and the holy Koran, which he claimed to have read no fewer than ninety-two times while walking along beside his camels. Any conversation with him was littered with quotations and he needed no excuse to deliver rambling and interesting lectures on the meaning of the passages he quoted.

He was equally loquacious about his camels and knew the breeding of every beast he had ever owned, back through ten or more generations. Although he had never received any formal education, he was able to deliver his discourses in five languages, including the most beautiful French. As a result I, along with all the other members of the caravan, many of whom had travelled with him before, was able to benefit from his wisdom.

During the evening when I joined the caravan, Mehmet Alu sauntered over and inspected my two camels. As he walked around, feeling a leg here and a joint there, he asked where I had bought them and, although I suspected he already knew it all, who I had bought them from and how much I had paid. For one of them, he said I had paid more than it was worth. The camel was probably nearer sixteen years old than the nine I had been told and, although she was presently producing milk, he was certain that after about ten days of desert travel she would be dry and start losing weight rapidly, however much fodder I gave her. The camel's name was Dji'emel, which apparently meant she was prone to scrawniness.

He suggested that when the caravan reached the T'imaali wells, where we would pause and rest for about four days, I should try to sell it for meat. At least that way I might recover a part of what I had paid. Leaving it any longer would not be a good idea as there wouldn't be enough meat left on the animal to make it worth eating and it was likely to die long before we were ready to leave Taoudéni, either to go onwards or to return to Timbuktu.

I was tempted to try and get rid of it there and then, but the assembly point was more than twenty miles from the camel market where I had bought it, the sun was already setting and the caravan would leave before dawn the next day. It was a hard lesson about the economics of desert travel. I would seek much more advice before buying, if I ever needed another camel.

My second camel, Améhan, pleased Mehmet Alu much more. He opined that she was a fine beast with many good breeding years ahead of her. She was only about four or five years old and had strong legs and good feet. Her joints were all sound and he liked the way she moved. Squeezing her teats, he squirted a brief jet of milk into the palm of his right hand, sniffed it and then tasted it. The look on his face was enough to tell me that he approved, but he treated me to a lecture on milk anyway.

Before he left me, Mehmet Alu asked if I would be returning to Timbuktu with the caravan, after the trading was done at Taoudéni, or whether I intended to continue northwards. I told him that I was going on to Oran in Algeria.

"Go to Laghouat, El Oued or Ouargala," he said. "Sell the

camel in one of those places. You will get a better price. I will send you to good men. One of them will buy her from you and not cheat on the deal."

He could see that I was puzzled by this and explained: "Laghouat, El Oued and Ouargala are all in the desert; the men there understand camels. When they know that you come from me, they will pay a fair price. If you take this camel to Oran, she will be wasted. The desert is her home; it is where she belongs." His hand caressed the animal tenderly as he spoke and I wondered if he would send me to a relation who would in fact be buying the camel for him. It seemed discrete not to ask, so I merely thanked him for his advice. He left me feeling that, although one of my beasts was suspect, I had actually done better in my first attempt at camel trading than he would have expected of a complete novice.

BELLOWING, SNARLING CAMELS, protesting at being loaded, or being made to rise with their heavy burdens of trade goods, woke me in the pre-dawn gloom. A few hot embers remained in my camp fire, so I added some pellets of dry camel dung and blew life into it. Within a couple of minutes I had a small kettle heating, for I was determined not to start this journey on an empty stomach. I had been warned by my companions that once the caravan set off we would not stop for at least sixteen hours. There would be little opportunity to prepare food on the move, so tea and some flat bread were essential.

While the kettle was heating, I packed the last of my baggage and loaded my two camels. The younger one carried the heavier load because for part of the day I would ride the older beast. If she was as unreliable as Mehmet Alu had indicated, and I saw no reason to doubt his judgement, it seemed fairer to let her carry a lighter load, at least for part of the time. Those who had done the trip before had warned me that it would only be practical to ride for about four hours during the hottest part of the day. Most people walked for the first five hours at this stage of the trip.

My kettle boiled as I finished tying on the second load. I mixed a little of the water and a drop of peanut oil with some flour and rolled out five small loaves of flat bread. Scraping the fire aside I laid these on the hot sand where the fire had been, brushed a little sand over the top and replaced the embers, adding two or three more pellets of camel dung to keep the fire going. The fire would give my bread a camelly aroma and flavour, but that was something I knew I would have to get used to. The rest of the hot water made tea which I drank while the bread baked.

Flat bread cooks quickly in hot sand and comes out with a gritty crust. My teeth would not thank me for the abrasive food they would have to chew for the next few weeks, but that's the way it is in the desert. I dusted off as much sand as I could and laid four loaves on a patch of rock to cool while I broke open the fifth and dunked it in my rapidly cooling tea. The air was very fresh just before dawn, with a slight breeze that gave it a sharp chill on your face. The breeze was not yet strong enough to pick up any grit, and would probably die down as the sun came over the eastern horizon, but this too was to become a feature of our mornings for the next month or so.

By the time I had eaten my breakfast loaf and drunk my tea, most of the other people nearby were prodding their camels to their feet and getting ready for departure. I put the remaining loaves into my goat skin *wawaga* that had come with me from Upper Volta, and tied it on to Dji'emel's load beside my kettle.

Somewhere in the distance a trumpet sounded. The sound carried distinctly on the cool desert air and caused a brief moment of silence, even among the gurgling snarling camels. Then everyone started to talk and to move at the same time. I stood my two beasts, tied Améhan's head rope to a loop on the broad strap that passed under Dji'emel's belly and, taking hold of the other head rope, followed those who were already moving off.

The sun didn't rise for another hour, but the pre-dawn gloom gave enough light to see where we were going as our eyes had accommodated to the darkness through the night. The stars were not yet beginning to fade and the half-grown crescent moon was still just above the horizon. I was unaware, as the caravan began its march, that I would see forty-three more dawn starts, not all as calm as this, before I next saw a town.

The group among whom I had camped the previous night were mostly Hausa traders, and a few Tuareg, who had come west from Niger and the northern states of Nigeria to join the salt caravan. Often the Tuareg remain aloof and keep themselves separate from people of the negro tribes, but coming from the same region had given them a shared identity and they obviously knew each other well from previous voyages, both on this and on other routes. They were a friendly bunch who apparently saw nothing strange in a lone white man joining their expedition. They thought it strange, however, that I was making the journey just for curiosity, in order to see the great salt mines and to share the experience of the caravan. They couldn't understand why I hadn't brought any trade goods with me. Nevertheless, they welcomed me into their group with the friendly acceptance of men who were widely travelled and accustomed to meeting folk from different cultures.

The ground beneath our feet was firm and the pace was

energetic until dawn. We must have covered a good four miles before the sun erupted over the horizon, transforming the land from a gloomy monochrome, through rich reds, fiery orange and golden yellow to bathe the fawn-grey desert in the glare of the newborn morning. It took barely half an hour for this transformation to be complete and soon afterwards the temperature began to rise.

The early breeze died with the arrival of dawn and for the next two hours the air warmed rapidly under the sun's radiance. By about nine o'clock, the air was stirring into motion as the rocky ground began to reflect the rays of the steeply rising heat source. Small thermals formed and, with them, minor twisting columns began lifting the lightest dust particles to form small willi-willies. At first these moved slowly across the open ground but soon collapsed when they encountered anything standing above the surface. By mid-morning, however, these micro-tornados turned more energetically, spinning fast and lifting heavier particles of grit that stung exposed skin when the willi-willies' wanderings brought them in contact with the meandering line of the caravan.

By late morning, the dust devils were strong enough to really hurt and men began to mount their camels. As I prepared to mount Dji'emel, I looked back to where the groups of women and children followed, driving their herds of fat-tailed sheep and goats. They were already riding, most on camels, a few on mules and only the eunuchs, slaves whose job it was to oversee and protect the women, were still on foot.

Mounting a camel on the move requires some skill which takes a lot of practice to acquire. Walking with the camel on the right, one has to pull downwards on the head rope to make the beast lower its head. The natural tendency of the camel when this is done is to lower the shoulders as well, so the curve of its neck is within reach of a raised right foot. Before the camel stops and kneels, the right foot must be planted on the animal's lowered neck as one springs upwards. Holding on to the saddle, you then have to swing your body round to land on top, hooking the right knee over the saddle horn. The left leg is then swung forward and across so that the foot is placed over the right leg, thus enabling you to grip the saddle between your knees. It all sounds fairly simple, but just try doing it, especially if the camel is not in a mood to be ridden. It is far from easy.

On this first morning, Dji'emel did not want to be ridden. She made this very plain when I tried to mount. As I pulled her head down, she swung it in a low arc to her left, her jaws gnashing, and tried to bite my kneecap. I skipped out of the way of her attack and she immediately raised her head and glared down at me imperiously from a great height, snarling and gurgling all the while.

I tried again, but she jerked her head, snatching the head rope out of my hand and wandered away to the right so that I had to run after her. This made my companions laugh and offer a selection of ribald comments on my performance as a camel jockey and on the suitability of my beast as a mount. The comments stung me; Dji'emel was not the first camel I had owned or ridden and I was normally much more competent than this. The beast was just not in the mood to be ridden and they all knew that. I was certain they had all had similar problems with a reluctant steed in the past. There was nothing for it but to halt, couch the beast and climb aboard while she was down.

As I was about to throw my leg over the saddle Dji'emel tried to rise and I had to whack her between the ears with my camel stick. She lowered her head, snarling, and settled back on the ground. Quickly I put a loop of rope round her left knee, with a slip knot that would allow me to release it once I was in the saddle. This was greeted with more snarling and gurgling and another attempt to take a chunk out of me, so I had to tap her neck with the stick again. As soon as the slip knot was tied, I leapt for the saddle, pulled the knot free and urged Dji'emel to rise.

She just sat there, looking smug, as my friends laughed and enjoyed my discomfort. One of them must have come up behind and poked Dji'emel in the rump, for she suddenly lurched forward and heaved herself to her feet with another angry bellow. I managed to hang on, but my friends had another good laugh at my expense. Looking back on it later, I was able to see the funny side, but at the time I just felt foolish and inadequate among these men who were so naturally competent.

While all this was going on, Améhan, my other camel, stood patiently waiting at the end of her lead rope. For the next half hour I drove Dji'emel hard and made her go where I wanted, not just to follow the animal in front, and hoped I was making it clear who was the boss. At first she resisted, but after a few judicious whacks with my bendy camel stick, she began to obey my verbal commands.

By this time the sun was very high. The glare reflecting off the rocky ground was intense and the breeze had steadied to about fifteen miles per hour. There is no doubt about it, the air was cooler atop a camel than it had been closer to the ground. Was this, I wondered, why camels walk with their heads held high, peering arrogantly down their noses at the rest of the world?

We rode until the sun was well past its zenith and visibly on the downward track. Before we dismounted, we came to a small patch of low dunes. They were composed of very soft, dry sand

and I could see the feet of the camels in front sinking deep into the stuff. I elected to stay in the saddle a little longer, aware that this light sand would be treacherous to walk in. Camel's feet are much better adapted to this sort of terrain and almost everyone else was still riding.

This band of dunes was about five miles wide but it took us nearly three hours to cross. The sand gave way once more to the hard rocky plain, which here had fewer dry water courses across it. With the sand behind us, I slid my foot down onto Dji'emel's neck, lifted myself forwards over the saddle horn and stepped down to the ground. The camel looked the other way and studiously ignored me. We walked on until three hours after sunset, stopping only when the moon crept above the eastern horizon.

The long string of camels clustered into groups when we stopped. These groups were scattered for over a mile along our route. We each unloaded the beasts in our charge, hobbled them with a short rope tied between the front legs, just above the fetlock, and then released them. I had been advised by Abdau Hamman, one of the Tuareg from Niger in whose group I was travelling, to tie my two animals' heads together with a short line. This would ensure that they were easier to catch in the morning and make them less likely to wander far or in different directions. He told me that his people often did this with new camels brought into their herds until they had established their place in the herd hierarchy.

Clumps of coarse grass grew not far from where we stopped and, the moment the animals were released, they headed for these. By the time we had lit our small flickering fires to make tea, the sounds of grass being ripped from the clumps echoed through the darkness. I filled a pan with water and set it to boil before adding some rice. I had one small loaf left from my breakfast bake and I chewed on this, dunking it in a mug of strong black tea, while I waited for my rice to cook.

As soon as their fires were lit and water had been set to boil, my companions turned east for their evening prayer. I noticed that many of the men, particularly those from the black tribes, did not join in the prayers. Once we were all settled and eating our food, I asked about this.

"Most of the slaves are heathens," came the reply from one of the Tuareg. "They have no faith and do not pray."

This took me slightly by surprise. I knew, of course, that there were still slaves among the desert people but I realised, with a mild feeling of guilt, that I had never really given the question much thought. It never occurred to me that there would be slaves on the salt caravan. The conversation that followed opened my eyes.

The salt trade depended heavily on slaves, both to mine the great slabs of salt from the lake deposits at Taoudéni and to load and transport them all across West Africa on the camel caravans. Many, if not most, of the Tuareg families kept slaves. They had done so for generations and their slaves formed an important part of the family's wealth. Most had been born into slavery, had never known freedom and had no concept of what it meant. Very few, as I discovered by talking to them over the next few weeks, had any desire to be free. Their owners were responsible for their food and clothing, for their protection and for looking after them if they were ill. There is no doubt that some of these people were abused and used in a harsh and undignified way, but this was not universally true. Among the Tuareg with whom I discussed the subject, there was strong disdain for anyone who neglected or abused his slaves. While they were seldom treated with the same level of care and affection as family members, they were seldom as mistreated as many may suspect. Some slaves commanded considerable respect for their wisdom, experience and skills and served as trusted and valued members of the family to which they belonged. Few would ever be sold for mere money.

In many cases, the only discernable difference between slaves and their owners was that the slaves owned nothing; both they and all the animals and goods in their care belonged to their owners.

The only time this became a problem was if an owner parted with one of his slaves, either in settlement of a debt, or because another wanted to acquire the slave to improve the breeding potential of his own slaves. The family break-ups that this caused could be the source of major discontent. In a settled community, where family contact could be maintained, this might not be so bad, but the Tuareg were nomadic and few stayed still for long, even if they did keep returning to familiar places. Once they moved on, they might be away for months or even years before returning to their starting point. Those in bondage had no option but to endure the pain such separation caused.

I asked Mehmet Alu about the slaves and how the system worked. Much of what I learned came from him. He was also proud that his people, the western Tuareg, took better care of their slaves and treated them with much greater humanity than some others. He was very critical of the tribes further east, particularly those in eastern Niger and Chad who, he told me, were cruel and wasteful of their slaves. It was not uncommon among those tribes for slaves to die of neglect or abuse because they were considered less than human. Among his people the slaves were recognised as people of worth, even though they were bonded and did not share the same rights as their masters. At the same time, he was quick to point out, they did not have any responsibilities. To Mehmet

Alu, his slaves were every bit as valuable as his camels and those to whom I talked said that he treated his slaves as well as he did his camels.

Almost all of the women and fully one-third of the men in our caravan were slaves. This gave me a lot to think about as we travelled. One day I asked Mehmet Alu what he knew about the historical involvement of Europeans in the slave trade. His reply was slightly dismissive and yet he was aware that Europeans had, in former times, made great trade in African slaves.

"The Faranj took men from the coastal tribes, but it was the black men themselves who sold their people," he said. "There are records in Timbuktu of slaves bought from the black tribes and taken across the desert to serve the caliphs in Khartoum and Jeddah, as much as six hundred years ago."

People were sold as servants by their own tribes in order to pay the trade duty they owed to their Tuareg overlords, he said, warming to his subject. This trade was particularly strong some time after the great empires of Mali, Songhai and Ghana had collapsed, when gold was no longer as plentiful as it had been. The black tribes also discovered that they could obtain European trade goods by selling slaves on the coast, but for a long time as many slaves were sent across the desert as ever went by sea and white men did not come to this desert until a hundred years ago. In time the desert trade became less profitable as Levantine traders took slaves from countries in the east that they could reach easily with their great ships. "Also our people travelled less far, so the trade dwindled. My own people have not traded slaves for two hundred years, but they are still an important part of every family's wealth."

After that lecture, I began to watch those men in the caravan whom I knew to be slaves and to talk to them when the opportunity arose. One of Mehmet Alu's slaves had heard him talking to me. I asked his permission to quiz the man and he shrugged, telling me to talk to whom I chose. The slave, Melo, was a tall man with very black skin and features that suggested he had Mandingo origins. I asked him where he came from.

"Nioro du Sahel, I was born one day's walk south of Nioro," he replied literally.

"What about your family?" I asked, realising that this was going to be a slow process. "Where did they come from?"

He shrugged. "Wherever Mehmet Alu or his father took them."

"Don't you have any tribal family?"

"Once, maybe," Melo said, looking slightly puzzled. "But that is so long ago it is forgotten. Mehmet Alu's family are my tribe."

"Do you not wish you had a family of your own?" I persisted.

"Mehmet Alu is my family," he said. "When I became a man, he gave me a wife and she has made two children with me. We are all his family."

"But he owns you like he owns these camels." I tried again. "Don't you ever want to have your own camels?"

He laughed. "I have all these camels. I look after them. They are mine. Why should I want others?"

"But Mehmet Alu could sell them and then you would have none."

"Of course. They are his to sell. Sometimes he asks me and I tell him which ones are best to sell, but he is wise. He can sell or buy what he likes."

"Do you ever want to buy anything?"

"If I think another camel is good for our herd, or if we need something, I tell Mehmet Alu. He will get it if he thinks it is right and the price is good. Sometimes he gives me money and tells me to buy something."

"Do you have any money of your own?" I asked.

"What for?" Melo seemed surprised at my question. "I have my work and my food; a tent to sleep in and clothes on my back. If I need something, Mehmet Alu provides it. Why do I need money?"

I looked carefully at Melo as he said this. He was clothed in a good robe and head cloth, with a warm blanket to wrap round himself at night and a pair of goat skin sandals that were easily repaired on the march and ideal for the desert. He had a good knife, a rifle in a soft leather case and a bandolier of ammunition. He had use of the communal cooking pots and food supplies. There was nothing else that he needed. He seemed genuinely happy and in no way resented the fact that his whole being was at another man's whim.

Over the next few weeks, I found that this attitude was prevalent among all the slaves I talked to. The only grumbles that I heard were of no consequence and not a single man resented being owned by his master. One or two did admit that they had previously received some harsh treatment, but said that this was not common and they had merited any beatings they received.

"What about the women?" I asked Melo.

"It is the same for them," he replied.

"But do they get used for sex by their masters?" I asked, wondering if this might be a touchy subject.

"Very seldom," Melo said. "The Tuareg do not like to mix their blood with black people. All the slaves are black. A woman may be given by her master to a different man, if he wishes to reward him, or because the master thinks she will breed good children, but that is only among the black slaves. It does not happen often."

"Do you get any choice of women, if there is one you particularly like?" I asked Melo.

"A man can always ask his master, then the master will decide. Mehmet Alu asked me who I wanted for a wife. He offered me a choice of three. I liked one of them and he made her my wife."

"What happens if another man wants your wife?"

"Unless Mehmet Alu gives his permission, the man may not touch her."

"But if he took her anyway?" I pressed the question.

"Mehmet Alu would kill him," Melo said blandly. "Nobody may touch his property without his permission."

It was amazing how matter of fact the whole business seemed when Melo talked about it like this. It was difficult to get my head round the idea that people could be owned and bred like camels and yet that is precisely what he was describing.

No doubt there were horror stories in this business too, but all the slaves I met, both on this caravan and later at the salt mines, were content with their lot and saw no reason to change it. None had any desire to be freed from slavery.

This of course contradicted what I had learned at school about the slave trade. Then again, we had never been taught that it was the Africans themselves who were selling their own kin into bondage and who made the greatest gains by doing so. The story I was now being told, from the inside, sounded very different.

FOR FIVE AND A HALF DAYS, we travelled across a small sand sea. There were dunes as far as the eye could see in gently curving waves of yellow sand. None of them was very high and the grains

Sea of sand: scorching by day, cold at night.

were quite large and moderately firm under foot. I had given up my western shoes in favour of a pair of goat skin sandals I had bought in the market at Timbuktu. These had broad flat soles which spread the load on the surface and left my feet free to flex. The sand slid out with every step instead of filling my shoes and this made walking far less tiring.

The sand sea was scorching by day and cold at night; the temperature fell by more than seventy degrees Fahrenheit from over 110 degrees to just a few degrees above freezing. We gathered a few sticks along the way, every time we came across any small bushes, and had brought a small amount of fuel with us. Together with the camel droppings collected by the slaves at the rear of the caravan, this gave just enough fuel to make tea and cook flat bread in the morning or, occasionally, rice and meat stew at night. There was not enough fuel for fires to keep us warm at night, so we huddled close together, wrapped in our blankets, and shivered.

Sunset in the sand sea turned the dunes from a pale yellow, through bronze to crimson before darkness descended. At dawn they turned from pale grey to gold and then a soft yellow in the cool of the few brief minutes it took the sun to rise clear of the horizon. Then, as the sun climbed swiftly into the empty sky, the colour faded to washed-out ochre that soon became hazy as the heat reflected off the surface. The dunes here were shallow, with no deep valleys between them, and so the small patches of shade were soon gobbled up by the advancing glare. Within an hour and a half, the night-time drop in temperature had been reversed and the scorching air passed the hundred degree mark on the thermometer I carried.

Crossing the sand, most of the men in the caravan rode for an extra couple of hours each day. This kept up the caravan's rate of travel because the camels' feet are better adapted to the soft terrain. The only ones who slowed were those at the back with the goats and donkeys. The half dozen Tuareg who normally chose to ride horses rather than camels, switched over to their camels and put broad soled bootees on their horses. With only their saddles to carry and this ungainly footwear, the horses, led by ropes tied to their master's camels, were able to keep up with the rest of the caravan. It was a simple bit of ingenuity.

NINETEEN DAYS AFTER leaving Timbuktu, we reached T'imaali Wells, a small oasis in the Erg Bou Guerra. Spread over perhaps half a mile of stony ground there were a dozen or so scrawny tamarisk trees and a couple of dying palms. There were also six shallow wells, with low stone walls around them and brackish water that tasted like Epsom salts. Long ago there had been watering troughs beside each well, but time, the indifference of those who used them, and the trampling feet of many thirsty animals had reduced them to relics, broken and unfit for purpose. Instead the men detailed to draw water used large metal bowls into which they poured a couple of a gallons at a time as the water was pulled from the well.

It was a tradition of this caravan that the animals should be watered first, before people drew water for themselves. A thirsty camel can easily drink more than twenty gallons of water in a few minutes, but this assumes there is no delay in providing the water. Lifting every gallon by hand in leaking leather buckets from wells twenty-five feet deep takes time, so watering four hundred and eighty camels and fifty horses, not to mention the diminishing number of goats and sheep, is a slow business. We had been there seven hours before the first people got any water.

Because water was fairly plentiful and easy to get at, the caravan master planned to pause here for two days. In that time he expected every animal to be watered twice and the caravan to go on its way with full water bags. Just as Mehmet Alu had predicted, Dji'emel had suffered greatly on the trek and it was obvious that she was not strong enough to face the next long march that would take us to Taoudéni. Mehmet Alu had told me how to go about selling the beast for meat when the time came and, after discussion with my Tuareg travelling companions, I decided that now was the time to do it.

I sought out the man in charge of provisioning the caravan and asked if he would buy the camel, telling him that Mehmet Alu had told me to speak to him. He looked slightly sideways at me and then asked to see the beast. Dji'emel was standing where I had left her, watered but too tired to move off with the other camels. The victualler walked all round her and then named a price that was slightly more than half what I had paid. I tried to look disappointed and said he was making me totally impoverished.

"And you will have to kill it and skin it for me," he added.

"But I am a *nasrani*," I said. "If I kill the beast, nobody will be willing to eat the meat."

"*Nasrani* or *musulman*, if you kill it in the proper manner they will eat," he replied.

"And what of the skin?" I asked.

"Do you think this is a charity that I run?" he sounded peeved. "Oh, all right, you can keep the skin. I will send my slave to see that you kill it properly and to collect the meat." With that he walked off.

A few minutes later his slave arrived, carrying a number of baskets and a long sharp knife which he presented to me, indicating that I should use this to slaughter the camel. Without a word, he laid out his baskets and then couched the camel and tied its foreleg firmly with a piece of rope from one of his baskets. Then he stood back waiting. I picked up the knife and tested the edge. It was well honed and would make a clean cut.

Slaughtering camels is a messy business and it takes some time for all the blood to drain before it is permissible to skin the carcass or to cut up the meat. I hated doing this because, despite her awkward nature, I had got used to Dji'emel and her quirky ways. We had maintained a daily battle of her trying to bite me while I skipped out of the way. This seemed a slightly unfair way to claim victory and end that relationship. At the same time, I could see that she was suffering badly and that every extra day I delayed this event was only going to make that suffering worse. I had no right to make her die in agony. In a perverse way she could still have an honourable end, as a piece of meat.

Once I had done the first bit, the slave joined in. He nodded to indicate his approval of the way I had done it and then helped me do the rest of the job. He had slaughtered many beasts and silently showed me exactly what he wanted done next. I had slaughtered sheep and goats before, but a camel is a different task. It took the two of us over an hour to clean and cut up the carcass. When I wanted to make string out of the intestines, as I would with a goat, he shook his head and insisted that that part of the offal be buried in the sand. As the last piece of the carcass was lifted off the skin, he cut off a good-sized lump of meat and placed it in my hand, making eating gestures. He handed me the sum I had agreed as the price of my camel, then he and some other slaves who had come to help picked up the laden baskets and returned to the victualler, who would then distribute the meat around the caravan.

It was sad to say goodbye to Dji'emel in this way but there was no acceptable alternative. My travelling companions told me that I had done the right thing and had received full value from the animal. This was the desert, there was no place for passengers or sentimentality here. Since the camel would undoubtedly have died anyway, why not get at least a good meal and a few francs out of my investment? Unpalatable though this was, I knew they were right.

THE NEXT AFTERNOON a sandstorm blew up. It lasted for three days. This was not the first sandstorm we had endured on this trip, but it was the most severe so far. The wind was laden with grit and dust, making it necessary to cover our mouths with several layers of cloth to avoid the choking muck. Any exposed skin felt as though it was being abraded by a hard pot scourer and it was almost impossible to see anything, even through sand goggles. Fortunately I had thought to bring a pair with me, although most people in the caravan didn't have them. Their only recourse was to cover their heads completely and stay still, crouched or sitting in huddled groups, relying on contact with the next person to confirm that the normal world still existed. The wind roared and howled, gusting fiercely and frequently changing direction as it did so. It was impossible to relax or sleep and any idea of preparing food or tea was completely out of the question.

The wind didn't even diminish when night fell, although the abrasive feel of it seemed to be less. This, my companions assured me after it was over, was purely an illusion that happened because by nightfall our bodies were so battered that all normal sensation was suspended.

Thirst was a real problem, because none of us could move far enough or easily enough to raise a water skin. For the first couple of hours, it was not so bad, because I had a two-litre metal water bottle with a screw cap. I passed this to the next person in our small group and each person took a sip before passing it on. They were not so selfish as to fully slake their thirst and the bottle made three full circuits over the first four hours before it ran out.

Most of the camels had been hobbled and released when we first stopped, but one or two were seated nearby. We could occasionally hear them gurgling, but they too had no alternative but to stay still and wait out the storm.

I must have lapsed into sleep once or twice during that storm, for I remember waking with a start on several occasions only to find that the nightmare was still in progress. I tried to look at my watch when daylight came the second time, but its crystal had been so abraded by the sand that it was opaque, making it impossible to see the hands.

When the storm first started and we were gathering our possessions together and piling them in the middle of our circle, I had pulled Dji'emel's skin over myself and the person on either side of me, with the fur inwards. We each took hold and wound loose flaps of it round our hands and feet, pulling the edge tight over our heads. This gave us some protection. The blasting grit lashed against the raw membranes coating the inside of the skin. In fact the storm did a cleaning job for me and scraped away all the fragile membranes and thin bits of fat that had been left on when the animal was skinned, leaving it much cleaner than it would have been had I worked it by hand.

When the storm finally abated, it was not a gentle process with the wind gradually decreasing, but a sudden stop, as though someone had thrown a switch and turned everything off. It took fully half a minute for us to realise that the storm had ceased and to raise our heads to look around. Then, gradually, the caravan came to life. Faint voices called to one another. Some were faint because they came from the other end of the oasis, others because our hearing had been so deadened by the roaring wind that anything less than a shout was temporarily inaudible.

It was early morning, about two hours after dawn and the air was only just heating up. Slowly people stood up and began moving about. During the morning, word came from the caravan master, passed from group to group, that we would stay another day at the oasis in order to water our camels, refill the skins and prepare a decent meal and some travelling food. Men set off to search for the camels, some of which had wandered away before the storm hit us. Some were nearby; others they met already returning in search of water. A few had gone further and would take a bit of searching to find.

"What happens if we cannot find some of them?" I asked Abdau Hamman.

"The men in charge of them will wait here," he replied. "The camels will come back in a week or so. They cannot go longer than nine days without water, so they will return to the last place they received water."

I looked around for Améhan, my remaining camel, but could see no immediate sign of her. I walked around the groups of beasts jostling for water beside the well heads but could not see a camel with the green head collar that Améhan had been wearing when I released her after her last watering. I was beginning to feel slightly feverish and returned to my campfire to make tea. By the time I had it brewed, my temperature was very high and I was shivering intermittently. Unless my camel came back of her own accord, or was brought back by one of my companions, I might have to stay here when the caravan moved on. My baggage had been unloaded before Améhan was watered so I had everything I needed, and there was water in the wells. I would be safe enough. Abdau Hamman told me a dozen or more people would probably be left behind, as thirty or forty camels were still unaccounted for.

At sunset, after sharing a meal of boiled goat and rice with the others, I settled down by my small fire, took a strong dose of anti-malarial pills in the hope that this was the fever I had, and curled up on the ground to try and sleep it off. When I woke at dawn, Améhan was couched a few feet away, with her left knee firmly bound. A slave from another group had seen and recognised her while out catching his master's camels. He had brought her back. Apparently my green head collar had been the subject of discussion up and down the caravan since we set out and everyone knew this was my camel.

"Who was the man?" I asked. "I should thank him for this kindness and maybe give him some reward."

"No reward is necessary; it is the way of caravan travellers to help one another. If you want to say anything, you should thank his owner," Abdau Hamman said. "He was only a slave, but think carefully first in case you incur some obligation that would be a disadvantage to you."

"What do you mean, obligation? And who is his owner?" I asked.

"You should have guessed," he said with a grin. "That slave's owner is Alhaj Mehmet Alu, the craftiest man in the caravan. If you thank him, he will assume that he has done you a service and therefore you owe him a service. I saw how he looked at your camel on the evening before we set out, and how he told you the best place to sell her. He wants that camel when you are ready to sell her. If you are under obligation to him he will expect to pay less."

"I hadn't thought of that," I said, feeling slightly foolish, but glad I hadn't just walked blindly into that situation. "But if I say nothing, that would be rude."

"Why? We all help each other with such things. It is taken for granted that one will bring back another man's camel if it is straying and can be caught. No man in this caravan would ever leave another stranded in the desert. You would do the same yourself," he protested. "Did anyone ask you to share your camel skin during the sandstorm? Did anyone make you pass round your water bottle when the wind was so strong we could not move to use our skins and would otherwise have been thirsty? No, you did it because the others are your companions and we all depend on each other. Anyway, you were asleep with a fever when the camel was brought back. You do not know who brought it or whether someone else told him to do that. Every man in this caravan knows your camel and would have done the same."

After this interesting and timely lesson in caravan etiquette, I took Améhan to the well to get her some water. I was feeling marginally better, but did not fancy sitting at this battered oasis for another week because my camel had wandered off. I still had some of the fodder I had brought from Timbuktu, so I fed her well, thinking I would have to lighten my baggage now that I only had one camel to carry everything.

According to my map, our route should have been only a degree or so west of due north and, as far as I could tell, this had been how we travelled. After the T'imaadi wells oasis, however, the caravan master led us much more to the west to get out of the sand. The desert became once more a place of rock and stone, with only very small deposits of sand and no significant dunes. Gullies and ancient water courses scarred the plain; lumpy outcrops of bare rock, blackened by the sun, looked menacing as they shimmered in the heat haze.

This stony desert was very different and it was as if we had come to another country. According to one of my companions, we very nearly had because this western route took us close to the Mauritania border. Not that anybody would have cared; this was empty desert and the only signs of life, apart from our caravan, were the occasional silvery lizards skittering swiftly over the scorching rock or the white lines of condensation trails left by the few airliners passing high overhead on their journeys from the West African coast to Europe. Otherwise we might have been on Mars or the moon. There weren't even any kites or vultures soaring high in the sky to relieve the monotony. There was, however, much more wildlife here although most of it remained unseen to the untrained eye.

The first valley we passed through was infested with small lizards and dull brown snakes. My companions warned me that the snakes were all venomous and took a delight in pointing them out. Some were coiled up and looked like knobbly bits of rock; others had embedded themselves in patches of sand, barely visible until they were stepped on. Then, like lightning, their head would dart out a couple of feet from where they were concealed as they struck.

Several of the camels got bitten and I noticed that some of the beasts were now wearing leather gaiters or bandages on their legs to protect them from snake bites. Fortunately the camels seemed relatively immune to the snake venom, but I was warned that men had died from being bitten and more than a few goats and sheep were lost on every trip. It was just one more of the hazards of desert travel.

At night when we stopped, a concerted effort was made to clear the ground all around our campsite. Any snakes we found we carried off and dropped several hundred yards away. Surprisingly nobody tried to kill them. When I asked why, I was simply told that it was too much effort. As long as they bit nobody, what harm were they doing? Such an attitude is not common in Africa, where most people are terrified of snakes and will always try to kill those they encounter, but these were desert men and the snakes were part of their environment. Life was hard enough here without the additional effort of hunting and killing snakes for no purpose.

We travelled much faster in this rocky region and within a day and a half, we turned northwards again. The camels seemed to have new heart too, almost as though they knew we were past the halfway point. This part of the journey still took us eleven days and we were not finished with sand yet.

We passed through a small patch of desert with a very different aspect. The land was sculpted by the grit-laden wind and, as well as rocks being eroded, there were some that had actually grown because of the wind-borne grit. These were huge structures like rocky sculptures of reddish yellow stone discs that had somehow become pressed together at odd angles and frozen in time. In most of these, the discs were small and the rocks had both a knobbly and an angular appearance at the same time. In others they were massive, with the discs the size of dinner plates. These were the famous desert roses. I had seen smaller examples before in the Mzab region of Algeria, but never imagined they could be as big as houses like some of these.

Nobody thought much about environmental damage in those days and I didn't even give the matter a second thought as I knocked a small piece off one of these fantastic and beautiful structures and stuffed it into my saddle bag as a memento. These desert roses are fragile structures and not difficult to break, but somehow it survived my travels.

A WEEK AFTER LEAVING the T'imaali oasis. we came down off a high rocky escarpment into a region of dunes laid out in long parallel ranks. Each dune extended, almost straight, as far as the eye could see toward the north-east. The caravan followed the trough between two dunes which rose about a hundred feet on either side. The ground in the bottom was firm and in places there seemed only to be a few inches of sand on top of bedrock.

We hadn't found water for a week and were very thirsty by the time we came to the next watering point. This was only a few days travel from our destination. The water quality was significantly different. Before it had been brackish; now it was definitely saline and, while it must have hydrated our desiccated bodies, it did little to slake our thirst. Even so, the camels drank greedily and I marvelled that their metabolism could take in so much brine and not be poisoned. When I made tea, I learned why the desert people put so much sugar in their tea and coffee, for it was quite undrinkable without it. Even the stew we ate that night was salty.

I wondered how the people who worked the mines managed. Most had been there for years and their kidneys must have been taxed to the limit to rid their bodies of the excess salt. It must have elevated their blood pressure to dangerous levels. Did they make an evolutionary adaptation, or did the salt simply poison their system until they died an early and unpleasant death? I suspected the latter and since almost everyone at the mines, including the overseers, was a slave, I don't suppose anybody cared.

We moved on two hours before dawn, on what was to be our last full day on the caravan route. Before midday, the dunes became smaller and we came to a roadway that had clearly seen recent wheeled traffic. We turned north-west and followed this for a few miles before we reached the first salt workings, but it took us a further four hours to reach the end of our journey. Along the way groups of traders peeled off from the caravan and disappeared into the broken countryside. Apparently there was not just one big mine, but many small sites spread across the vast ancient lake bed, each representing a different mining concession. Dozens of concessions were clustered around two or three bigger mines whose workings had become vast holes in the ground, but very few of them were obvious. This was because most of the mining went on below the surface in shallow caves excavated to protect the workers from the intensity of the sun.

The salt lake at Taoudéni was formed millions of years ago, long before the Atlas mountains to the west were pushed up and when the area was inundated by the sea. Gradually with tectonic movements the land rose and was eventually cut off from the sea, but not before deep deposits of salt had been laid down over a time span of a million years or so. In time the land rose and dried out, leaving a vast dry salt lake with an area of more than two hundred and forty square miles. Old records in Timbuktu dating from the 1500s tell of the salt being mined there and traded across the desert for at least the last six hundred years. Over that time, while miners have excavated many thousands of tonnes and their activity has scarred the surface, they have removed less than a hundredth of one per cent of the available salt.

HERE I DISCOVERED another aspect of slavery that had hardly been discussed during our conversations on the march. All the workers in the mines were slaves; some of them had arrived here as convicts, usually condemned for political crimes, which made them slaves of the state in a desert Gulag. Many of them wore heavy iron collars and even leg irons, joined by a short chain that made walking difficult. The treatment they received from the overseers was far from benign and their life expectancy cannot have been long in consequence. Their former identities were lost now and few admitted to their original names, even if one managed to persuade them to speak. Some could not speak for their tongues had been removed as part of their punishment and most had been tortured before being condemned to the mines.

Once here, their food was minimal and of inferior quality, their clothing insufficient to keep them warm during the cold nights and they received no medical attention whatsoever. There were said to be nearly two thousand convict slaves working the mines when I was there and they were a sorry sight. The guards were hard task masters. Usually black tribesmen from the south, they had neither interest nor care for human dignity and gave no scrap of kindness. When I wanted to take photographs, they became very hostile and I was obliged to retreat.

Before sunset on the evening we arrived, Mehmet Alu rode over to where our group had camped. With his white robes billowing in the evening breeze, he looked the archetypal desert icon in the late sunlight. He appeared like a vision from the pages of those romantic scribes who eulogised the noble desert nomads, resplendent on a magnificent white horse, riding off to do great deeds of daring and honour like desert versions of Sir Lancelot.

Sadly the reality was far from this. Yes, he was riding a white horse, and his robes were billowing in the evening breeze with the lowering sun at his back. There, however, the romantic similarity ended. His robes were travel stained and badly frayed at the edges. The horse was scrawny, dusty and in need of a good grooming and a decent meal. It's tack was worn, much repaired and hadn't been cleaned since we left Timbuktu, and there were dirty green patches below its eyes and nostrils where a slave had plastered it with a foul-smelling ointment to keep away the flies. In this he failed and the animal was accompanied by a cloud of buzzing flies which Mehmet Alu continually swept aside with a horsehair fly whisk.

The noble nomad himself was nothing more than a wrinkled old man, tired after a long, strenuous journey. He drooped over his steed's withers and clutched the saddle horn tightly with one hand to keep himself upright. I took hold of the horse's bridle as he stopped and a slave scuttled over to help him dismount and seat himself on a padded blanket in front of our fire.

Once the courtesies had been observed, he enquired about my plans now that we had reached our destination. He said that if I intended to carry on northwards into Algeria, I would have to go and visit the local administrator and inform him. Permission was not always granted for the northward crossing, because of political difficulties. However, at present relations were good and, since the British were generally welcome in Algeria, he did not expect me to be refused.

The administrator had been forewarned that I was with the caravan and readily agreed to my onward journey, although he clearly thought I was mad for undertaking such a journey without a sound commercial purpose. He issued me the necessary documents, charged me 450 Malian francs for the privilege (thirty-eight pence) and wished me "bon voyage".

When I returned to the encampment, Mehmet Alu was still there, chatting to Abdau Hamman and the others and sipping coffee. He was pleased that I had got my papers and then offered to buy my remaining camel from me.

"But how shall I make the crossing if I sell you my only camel?" I asked him.

"I will pay you now; you will take one of my slaves with you as far as Laghouat or El Oued or Ouargala and get a car or a truck from there to take you to the coast," he said in a slightly offhand manner. "A camel is not good transport after those places. The slave will bring Améhan back to me." He sipped his coffee and looked at me, letting his proposal sink in before he made a cash offer.

I noted that he had spoken of Améhan by name, not merely as

'your camel' and took this as an indication of the seriousness of his offer. Abdau Hamman had been right when he said that Mehmet Alu craved my camel. Perhaps this gave me a small advantage when the discussion came round to the price he should pay.

When, a few minutes later, he named the price he was prepared to pay, it surprised me greatly because it was more than I had paid for the camel in the first place and I was aware that he knew this. Also I still had a good few hundred miles to travel with her if I accepted his offer.

We haggled, of course, for to have done otherwise would have been to insult him. He improved the offer slightly and by the time we shook hands on our deal, he had agreed to almost the same sum that I had paid for both my camels in the market outside Timbuktu. Since the victualler had also paid me for Dji'emel when she was slaughtered, this made more than adequate compensation.

Mehmet Alu asked how long I would pause at the Taoudéni mines before continuing my journey. I had intended to stay for at least a week and explore the place, but what I had seen during the afternoon had been enough. Taking a sip of coffee made with salty water confirmed my change of mind on the instant.

"I have many miles to travel and my free time is getting short," I said. "I shall leave the day after tomorrow."

"Then come and eat with me tomorrow at sunset," Mehmet Alu invited me graciously. "I shall pay for Améhan then and give you the slave who will accompany you." So saying, he took his leave and returned to his own encampment a satisfied man.

Abdau Hamman looked at me speculatively and asked, "Is it really true that you are not a habitual trader of camels?"

"Of course I'm not. I'm a water engineer," I said, surprised at his question. "Why do you ask that?"

"Because either you have just made the best bargain in a century of camel trading, or Mehmet Alu is finally losing his senses," he laughed. "He has paid you four times what that beast is worth, and we all know it," he said waving his hand round to indicate our travelling companions. "And you haggle like a Niamey market trader!" The others all laughed and I accepted his compliment with a bowed head.

The meal Mehmet Alu gave me the following evening was a veritable feast with fresh goat meat, rice with pistachios, cashews and almonds in it; cinnamon couscous with sheep's butter and honey and a sauce made with the juices from the roasted goat. He also gave me date wine and when I expressed surprise that he also drank this, he smiled.

"The Prophet, all peace be upon him, forbade drunkenness, not wine," he said. "In his time, it was not safe to drink much of the water because of diseases, so wine was normal. The alcohol killed the diseases. But excess, as with anything, is forbidden. In time this became a rejection of all alcohol in order to help the weak-willed not to disgrace themselves, and so it is today. But to take a small drink of wine is nothing more that to offer respect to Allah's limitless bounty."

We had been served throughout the meal by a wizened little man with a very black skin who wore a smart green turban. When we had finished eating and coffee had been served, Mehmet Alu called the man forward, told him also to take coffee with us and to sit. He introduced the man as Amilu, the slave who was to accompany me on my onward journey and bring Améhan back. He was one of Mehmet Alu's most trusted men and very knowledgeable about camels. He had been to both Laghouat and Ouled Djelal many times before and knew the way well. He also spoke good French.

Sitting here in the desolate northern wastes of Mali while being entertained like an honoured guest by this extraordinary old man, I thought back to the times I had been given supper by a number of Africa's heads of state including, some years previously, the President of this country. Mehmet Alu may not have been a national president, but he was certainly a man of far greater stature and wisdom than many. Besides being a tough desert nomad, skilled in the management of trading caravans and all that they involved, he had managed to accumulate a vast store of education and wisdom which crossed cultural divides with ease. He had a clear perspective on world issues too often clouded in the minds of lesser men.

Although his son was now the caravan master, Mehmet Alu was the head of his own trading empire. As I was to discover later, thousands of miles to the east, his name and reputation spanned the whole Sahara and much of the Middle East besides. It struck me that I was once more having 'supper with the President'.

We had eaten well and when we had drunk three small cups of black coffee infused with juniper berries and cardamom seeds, I offered my thanks for the meal and all Mehmet Alu's courtesy and help during the march northwards. He reached inside his robe and pressed a package into my hand. This, I knew, contained his payment for Améhan, so I touched it to my lips and forehead in recognition of his generosity. Putting the packet in my pocket, I took my leave of him and Amilu accompanied me back to my own encampment.

WE LEFT TAOUDÉNI AND its vast salt mines before dawn the next day, just the two of us and three camels. We walked for two days before we got clear of the ancient dried salt lake and into 'normal' desert, and then travelled hard for a further week, walking and riding, moving for at least sixteen hours a day until we finally arrived in Laghouat forty-seven days after leaving Timbuktu.

At Laghouat, Amilu and my camel, Améhan, turned back and I hitched a ride on a truck belonging to one of the contractors working in the oil and gas fields that was going up to Oran on the Mediterranean coast. The engine was loud, the driver spoke little French and I found his Arabic difficult to understand; it was a noisy, smelly, uncomfortable twenty-six hour journey. Despite all that the desert had thrown at us, I felt intense sadness leaving behind its tranquillity, the amiable chatter of my companions and the steady rhythm of the camel train.

Glossary

atelier – A workshop. This term comes from French, but has been adopted by many of the African languages in the countries that were formerly French colonies. In some cases an *atelier* is a proper workshop; more often it is a space under a tree where an artisan has his tools and plies his trade. The tools are usually basic, much adapted by the village blacksmith, or even home made.

balafon – A traditional xylophone made with dried gourds hanging beneath the percussion slats to provide a muffled musical resonance. Some are constructed as a frame that is carried on a shoulder strap with the percussion slats supported on thongs above and the gourds hanging below, others are made as free standing frames and look more like the western concept of a xylophone.

baobab – The African baobab, *Adansonia digitata*, is often referred to as the 'Tree that God turned upside down' or, in some areas, the 'Tree of Life'. This grotesque and long-lived inhabitant of the African bush has many uses and as many taboos and myths associated with it.

bidonville – The tin shanty town surrounding most of the cities of French West Africa. The huts or houses are made from anything available, but most often along the Dakar railway line people used old forty-gallon oil drums (*bidons*). Tops and bottoms are removed; they are then split vertically, beaten flat and laced together to form the walls or roof panels. The resulting hovels are crammed together with neither sanitation nor regular water supplies.

CFA *francs* – Most of the former French colonies of West Africa belong to an economic union and use a common currency, the CFA franc. At the time when the events described in this book took place, the exchange rate was 630 CFA francs to £1. Mali alone used its own currency, the *Malian franc, FM* (qv).

colons – A mildly abusive term used to describe people from former colonial nations. The same word is used throughout French-speaking Africa and is often applied to any white man whose manner reminds people of their former colonists.

djellabia – The ankle-length garment, like a white or sand-coloured night-shirt, that is worn by many men throughout the Muslim world. It is cool, comfortable and well-adapted to desert life. When laundered and pressed, a *djellabia* looks smart, but when grubby or creased, it can look very scruffy. In some places this garment is also referred to as a *grand boubou*, literally 'big shirt'.

FM – *Francs Maliens*. Mali retained its own currency when the rest of French West Africa joined a common currency union and used CFA francs (qv). The Malian franc exchanged at 1,200 FM to £1, making 1FM slightly more than half a CFA.

fou-fou – The name used across most of West Africa for the root-based starch that forms the staple diet of much of the population. It is generally a smooth, porridge-like paste made from any one of a variety of different tubers, including yams, cassava (manioc), taro and sweet potato. In each case, the tubers are peeled, washed, boiled and then mashed in a large wooden mortar. In some areas the tubers are grated after the first cooking to make the mashing easier. The resultant pulp is then steamed until the texture is just right and the starch is cooked.

Fou-fou is eaten with the fingers, often with a wide variety of sauces, grilled meat or fish, stews – when meat or stockfish is available – and vegetables which are usually either spiced or loaded with hot peppers.

gecko – Small pink, almost translucent lizards that inhabit people's houses all over Africa. They feed on flies and other insects and have an uncanny ability to cling to any surface, even upside down, with feet that appear to have little round pads on the end of the toes. Other varieties of gecko grow bigger, some reaching almost eighteen inches long. These often have rough, knobbly skin and may be quite decorative, but with muted colours. These large geckos are not to be touched, for they have jaws like gin-traps.

gri-gri – This is the name for black magic in most of the former French colonies. In other parts of Africa it is often called *ju-ju* and has many other localised names as well. Magic takes many forms and is practised at different levels by sorcerers, witch doctors, witches, griots and other mysterious people, all of whom have been initiated into their secret art after long and demanding training. Their position is hereditary among many tribes. Many of the feats that these people can perform defy the explanations of western science but are nonetheless real and have great power in traditional culture. Despite their common scepticism, Europeans are far from immune to, or safe from, the effects of this magic, even though many believe that most of it depends of clever illusions and hypnotic hallucination.

gula mba'a – A traditional stew of fish and fowl with a few vegetables and lots of *pili-pili* (tiny hot chillies) in it. This is Madame Mobutu's recipe (makes enough for four people):

Ingredients:
Either 350g of dried stockfish or one large catfish steak (about 400g before removing bones and skin) cut into four pieces.
Half a chicken, with the bones removed, cut into pieces.
1 large tin* of fresh coconut milk or 1 packet of dried coconut cream.
1 large tin of soaked pigeon peas.
1 small tin of soaked cow peas.

* The two tin sizes are used all over Africa as standard measures for grains, powders and liquids. A large tin is the standard 400g tin, such as baked beans are packed in, and a small tin is the drum-shaped tin that contains fifty cigarettes.

1 small tin of soaked black eye beans.

1 large strong onion, cut coarsely.

2 large firm beefsteak tomatoes, cut into 6 large pieces each.

1 fresh mango, stoned and cut crossways into fingers.

Half a fresh pineapple, skinned and diced small.

4 whole fresh green hot chillies, split in half lengthwise, with the seeds left in.

300g fresh baby okra.

Half a small sweet pepper, sliced.

1 small can of Harissa hot pepper sauce made from pili-pili.

Method:

Boil the soaked pigeon peas, cow peas and black eye beans in water, without salt, until they are cooked. This takes at least half an hour.

In a separate large pan, bring the coconut milk to the boil and add the chopped onion, the fish and the chicken. Simmer for 10 to 15 minutes. Add the tomatoes, the chillies and the sliced sweet pepper. Make sure the chillies remain whole and do not get broken up. Stir gently and add a little water if the mixture is too dry. Add up to half the can of Harissa and stir in. (This will make it *very* hot.)

When they are cooked, drain the combined beans and add them to the pan, together with the mango and the pineapple and any of their juice that has come out in preparation. Stir well and simmer for 10 to 15 minutes, adding a little water if necessary.

10 minutes before serving, add the fresh baby okra. This should be crisp and not slimy when serving.

Just before serving remove the whole chillies.

Serve with *fou-fou* or maize porridge, rice or couscous.

A similar dish is made in Liberia, but there the fish and fowl are not mixed and the quantity of chilli paste is doubled, making it all but inedible.

kapok tree – A tall hardwood tree, *Eriodendron anfractuosum*, that has a trunk and branches heavily studded with short sharp thorns. The lowest branches are normally twenty feet or more above ground and the base of the trunk usually has heavy root buttresses rising to six feet or so. These trees produce seed pods containing a fine downy white fibre (kapok) in which the seeds are embedded. In many parts of West Africa, particularly in the coastal regions, kapok trees have special significance to sorcerers and witch doctors, the spaces between their buttresses being used for fetish altars at which to make offerings and sacrifices. In some places the trunks are used to carve dug-out canoes.

kola nuts – The fruit of the kola tree, *Cola acuminata*. They grow in large pods, each nut dividing into four lobes when the pod and the pink skin are removed. The nuts have a slightly waxy feel and a crisp, crunchy texture with a bitter, astringent taste that is probably caused by their nicotine content. The flesh changes colour when crushed and is chewed, but not swallowed, for its mild narcotic effect. When it has been well-chewed, the pith becomes bright red and leaves the mouth, gums and teeth stained the same shade. Until recently, the majority of the West African kola nut crop grew in Côte d'Ivoire, but its popularity in other countries has led to some cultivation in Nigeria and Cameroon.

mundele – Literally, a white man. The same word is used in many of the languages of central Africa.

pirogues – The canoes used by the fishermen on Lac Togo, they took two forms. The older ones were dugout canoes, hewn from large *kapok trees* (qv) when the area was still surrounded by tropical forest. They were heavy, between fifteen and eighteen feet long, with blunt ends. There were comparatively few for these left in the 1970s.

The newer boats were sleek, planked canoes, about twenty feet long and three feet wide. Many had cheap Japanese outboard motors on them and they were frequently painted in bright colours with faces, toothy jaws, or big eyes on their bows. These new *pirogues* were much faster in the water and more stable for the fishermen to work from.

sokago – The West African name for the wandering sickness. It has other names in other regions, but the symptoms are the same. Some say that *sokago* is induced by sorcery; others claim that it is a form of naturally occurring madness where a man's attention gets fixed on some fleeting image or spectre such that he feels an overwhelming compulsion to see it again. This compulsion can be so strong that he forgets what he is doing and follows the disappearing spectre, pursuing it obsessively to the exclusion of all rational activity. In this almost trance-like state, a man can wander for many days and cover great distances; when found, he will be bewildered and unaware of either where he is, where he came from or how he got there.

wawaga – A single-piece goat skin bag, made without cutting the skin open at the belly, so that the only opening is the neck. The legs are tied together by the hocks to form shoulder straps. Most commonly the fur is removed and the leather is cured to a soft suede-like texture. A wawaga is used for carrying any dry materials from grain or flour to household goods, clothing or small trade items.

Another version of the same type of bag, *imnuwaga*, usually with the fur left on the outside and with the leather treated to make it waterproof, is sometimes used as a water carrier or for milk.

Zaïres – The currency of Zaïre, renamed by President Mobutu in 1972 as part of his 'authenticity' programme. Naturally, the banknotes bore his image, the exception being the twenty MaKuta note which instead had the face of Patrice Lumumba, the first prime minister after independence and the man who made Mobutu his chief of staff and head of the Congolese army. There were a hundred MaKuta to the Zaïre and a hundred Senghis to the LiKuta, although no coin smaller than a ten Senghi piece was ever minted and few of these coins were circulated. The exchange rate in the 1970s was about £1.20 to 1Z.

Acknowledgements

SO MANY PEOPLE contribute to a book like this in a variety of different ways that it is difficult to name them all, but I am grateful to each and every one nonetheless, whether their contribution is evident or not. For those who have already joined the ancestors, I hope my words will stand as a small memorial to remarkable people I have known and remember as good friends. To the rest I say a heartfelt "Thank you" for their help, advice, criticism, encouragement, support and many other contributions.

Some stand out for particular mention. Among them are Jenny and Alan Brand, for reading my text and telling me when it didn't make sense. Gay and Lynne did sterling work proofreading and bringing a critical eye to bear on consistency with spelling and names.

Thanks to other writing friends around the world who have been generous with encouragement and maintaining my belief in what I was doing, among them Rosanne Dingli, Wendy Reis and Sylvie Nickels, whose own writings gave me standards to aspire to.

Sincere thanks also to my editor and publisher, Chuck Grieve, for his infinite patience and can-do approach; making the task of preparing a book for publication seem straightforward and easy, even when it involves a lot of hard work, and also for the many good cups of coffee which fuelled our working meetings.

Finally, special thanks to my lovely wife, for her patience when I was writing, her nagging when I was working too hard, and for always being there and providing the most wonderful support. I couldn't have done it without you.

Lightning Source UK Ltd.
Milton Keynes UK
UKOW020948250911

179261UK00001B/3/P

9 781906 852108